T0194995

The Seven Spirits of God

A New and True Revelation

D.W. Knight

WESTBOW
PRESS®
A DIVISION OF THOMAS NELSON
& ZONDERVAN

WestBow Press books may be ordered through booksellers or by contacting:

WestBow Press
A Division of Thomas Nelson & Zondervan
1663 Liberty Drive
Bloomington, IN 47403
www.westbowpress.com
1 (866) 928-1240

Scripture taken from the King James Version of the Bible.

ISBN: 978-1-9736-3708-0 (sc)
ISBN: 978-1-9736-3709-7 (e)

Library of Congress Control Number: 2018909816

Print information available on the last page.

WestBow Press rev. date: 8/22/2018

This book is dedicated to my heavenly Father, to Jesus Christ my Lord, and to the Holy Spirit who is the seven Spirits of God before his throne.

Introduction

As I sat on the second floor back porch of the house where I lived, I began a quest to read the Book of Revelation. I was a new believer and I had not read the entire Bible yet, especially the last book in the Bible which is the Book of Revelation. I was told by someone that it was a scary book and that it was full of symbolism and hard to understand. I decided to take on the challenge and read it anyway. I remember, I had heard the following scripture read at church at some point;

> Revelation 1:3 KJV
> Blessed is he that readeth, and they that hear the words of this prophecy, and keep those things which are written therein: for the time is at hand.

I wanted to be blessed, and I loved to read so I set out to read the entire book of Revelation. It was such a wonderful experience that I will probably never, ever forget it. The Holy Spirit ministered to me in a way like never before. I then realized one of the most important things that I could have ever learned in my life as a believer and that was if we stay with God, in the end, we win! We have the ultimate victory. At some point though, I noticed that there were a few scriptures that I thought contradicted some passages that I had previously read in the Bible. Notice how I said "I thought". In my own mind I came up with this conclusion. The Lord did not tell me this. I quickly learned later that the Word of God never contradicts itself, it does have contrasts but it never contradicts.

One of those incidences was the scriptural mention of the "seven Spirits of God". I noticed within the first five chapters of the book of Revelation that the seven Spirits of God were mentioned 4 times. Now, I had read another scripture (Ephesians 4:4), and I was also taught that there was only "one Spirit", and now I am reading about seven Spirits (these were my thoughts, I was a spiritual babe at the time). I was a bit confused but I still trusted what I was reading to be the truth and I knew in my heart that even though I did not understand what I had read, that fact didn't make the Word of God untrue. So I decided to let it be one of the many concepts in the Bible that I did not understand hoping that I would have a better understanding sometime in the future. Eventually the Holy Spirit revealed many precepts, principles, and concepts to me, but the revelation of "what" or "who" the seven Spirits of God were escaped my mental grasp and understanding.

One day I was reading one of the passages that mentioned the seven Spirits of God and I saw a cross reference in my Bible that led me to Isaiah chapter 11;

Isaiah 11:1-2 KJV
And there shall come forth a rod out of the stem of Jesse, and a Branch shall grow out of his roots: And the spirit of the LORD shall rest upon him, the spirit of wisdom and understanding, the spirit of counsel and might, the spirit of knowledge and of the fear of the LORD;

"Now" I said, I finally thought I had it. But, the Holy Spirit let me know I wasn't totally on the right track. I knew in my spirit that I was missing something. So I counted and found only six. I knew by the Holy Spirit that in the passage, the phrase "Spirit of the Lord" was not included with the six (which would make it seven). But, I knew that the six were an expansion of and part of the phrase "the Spirit of Lord". I had also learned by the Spirit that I could not entirely trust cross references and commentaries.

Cross references and commentaries are good for Bible study purposes but, they are only a Bible study tool. They bring you to a point where (if you use them correctly) you can get true revelation. But, they should be treated as a "study help" only. They are not the final authority. I have several of them in my library. The Holy Spirit has shown me many things through the help of cross references and commentaries. But I still needed to understand that I could not solely rely on anything but the Word of God and revelation from the Spirit of God.

Sometimes we elevate what people say or write or even

what "we" think in our own mind over what the Word of God has to say. The Word of God has the final authority. The Bible says the Holy Spirit – the Spirit of Truth will show us the truth but we must trust in his leading. If I want to understand the Word, I must go to the one who is the inspiration for every word that is written in the Bible, the Holy Spirit.

The Lord told us he would bless us if we read and keep or do the words of the prophecy. How can we do the Word if we can't understand it?

> Proverbs 4:7 KJV
> Wisdom is the principal thing; therefore get wisdom: and with all thy getting get understanding.

So, as I study the Word I expect to get revelation knowledge because I know he wants us to keep his Word. If I don't understand, I'll ask for it and he gives it all to me in his timing. He loves me and he wants me to know his Word. This has helped me in my quest to have a full and balanced understanding of God's Word.

When we look at the Word, we see things that are very specific. When you get revelation knowledge and understanding of the Word, sometimes certain points seem minute or minuscule until you look at the big picture. But, the Lord keeps adding to your understanding a little bit at a time until you are able to totally grasp it (Isa. 28:9-11).

So, the cross reference that led me to Isaiah 11:2 wasn't totally correct and I knew it. But as we will see later the cross reference wasn't totally incorrect. Years later

I eventually received a revelation of the seven Spirits of God which I am going to share with you prayerfully and reverently by the Holy Spirit. This revelation is not just good reading it is powerful truth that is needed by the body of Christ today in order for us to accomplish the work that he has called us to in these last days.

I'd just like to add that my teaching style incorporates a weaving in and out of connecting subjects. So there are times throughout this book that you will see this in the writing. Please be patient as you are reading because there is always the big picture and Gods Word is always interconnected and interrelated. The apostle Paul and others did the same as they wrote the scriptures inspired by the Holy Spirit. God Bless you.

The Revelation of His Sevenfold Glory

Revelation 1:4 KJV
John to the seven churches which are in
Asia: Grace be unto you, and peace, from
him which is, and which was, and which is
to come; and from the seven Spirits which
are before his throne;

As I sat at my desk studying the Word, I decided to begin
a detailed study in order to find out what the seven Spirits
of God were. I took my concordance and looked up every
scripture passage that had the words "the spirit of" within
its contents. Then I wrote down each scripture that
seemed to fit the criteria I had in my mind. It would have
been easy if there were only seven, but of course there
weren't "only" seven. I had to do an extensive search of
the Word to come up with about a dozen references (in
order to get revelation you have to dig and rightly divide
the Word). So I ended up narrowing it down to 11 or 12
or something close to that number, but I still wasn't sure
which ones were in or out. This brought much frustration
to me while I tried to figure this thing out in my head (you

can't figure the Word of God out in your head). We need revelation knowledge to see and understand God's Word; this is why it was troubling to me.

This was a season of great frustration for me. I had financial issues, along with the fact that I had been a pastor for only a few years and I had the care of the church on my shoulders. On top of all that I had been having some personal issues that I was dealing with at the time. When I look back at where I was emotionally and spiritually at that time, I would not have expected anyone (let alone myself) to get such a profound revelation of the Word that I was bound to receive.

End the end praise God, I received breakthroughs in every single area that I was having trouble with in that season. God delivered me with what seemed like a snowball effect. Once I received the first breakthrough the rest seemed to come swiftly.

I continued to seek the Lord and prioritize the study of his Word in spite of what I was going through at the time. And then I saw it, I saw the key. I can't exactly remember all the details that led up to it but I think the events happened in this order; I decided by the leading of the Spirit to study the following passages.

> Revelation 3:1 KJV
> And unto the angel of the church in Sardis write; These things saith he that hath the seven Spirits of God, and the seven stars; I know thy works, that thou hast a name that thou livest, and art dead.

Revelation 5:6 KJV
And I beheld, and, lo, in the midst of the throne and of the four beasts, and in the midst of the elders, stood a Lamb as it had been slain, having seven horns and seven eyes, which are the seven Spirits of God sent forth into all the earth.

Who has the seven Spirits of God? Jesus of course, he is the Lamb. The Word says he has the Spirit without measure (John 3:34). So I went back to the vision that John saw of the Son of Man (who is Jesus Christ). That's when I began to study his sevenfold glory in the following passages.

Revelation 1:12-16 KJV
And I turned to see the voice that spake with me. And being turned, I saw seven golden candlesticks; And in the midst of the seven candlesticks one like unto the Son of man, clothed with a garment down to the foot, and girt about the paps with a golden girdle. His head and his hairs were white like wool, as white as snow; and his eyes were as a flame of fire; And his feet like unto fine brass, as if they burned in a furnace; and his voice as the sound of many waters. And he had in his right hand seven stars: and out of his mouth went a sharp twoedged sword: and his countenance was as the sun shineth in his strength.

In the vision that the Apostle John saw, he turned and saw what I believe was an angel that looked like the Lord Jesus. He said in verse 13, he saw "one LIKE unto the Son of man". John knew what Jesus looked like, but this view of the Lord was different. How do we know it was an angel? Jesus said it in the following verse:

> Revelation 22:16 KJV
> I Jesus have sent mine angel to testify unto you these things in the churches. I am the root and the offspring of David, and the bright and morning star.

I believe we all may have angels that look like us. I'm not dogmatic about this but this scripture seems to support what I am saying. John saw the Lord's angel and when he saw him he noticed a sevenfold manifestation of his person.

Now let's examine verses 14, 15, and 16 in more detail.

> Revelation 1:14-16 KJV
> His head and his hairs were white like wool, as white as snow; and his eyes were as a flame of fire; And his feet like unto fine brass, as if they burned in a furnace; and his voice as the sound of many waters. And he had in his right hand seven stars: and out of his mouth went a sharp twoedged sword: and his countenance was as the sun shineth in his strength.

Now, the Holy Spirit highlighted verses 14-16 to me because they contain the sevenfold manifestation of his glory or the sevenfold glory of his being. Verse 13 does speak of his garment and his girdle (belt). But if you will notice, a garment and belt can be changed at any time but the other attributes are unchangeable. They are seven manifestations of his person. This is the sevenfold dimension of the glory of Jesus Christ. Let's look again at the list but, this time we are going focus on his physical attributes by specifically numbering them.

1. His head and hair
2. His eyes
3. His feet
4. His voice
5. His right hand
6. His mouth
7. His countenance (face)

The Lord showed me on that day the key to the revelation of the seven Spirits of God. All we had to do was look at the person of Jesus in the first chapter of the book of Revelation. Revelation 5:6 says that Jesus has the "seven horns and seven eyes which are the seven Spirits of God".

Throughout of the rest of this book I am going to attempt to give a basic but somewhat detailed summary of the revelation that I received for each of the seven Spirits of God. My main focus here is to give a solid reason why I believe the scriptures (Rev. 1:14-16) correlate with each of the seven Spirits of God that he has revealed to me.

This is the basic revelation the Holy Spirit gave me when he showed me each of the seven dimensions of the seven Spirits of God. Now remember, these are summaries of each dimension of the Spirit. Each one of the seven Spirits of God can end up as an entire book individually. Later on in the book I will give you more revelation that is connected with the seven Spirits of God which is an entire body of revelation that the Holy Spirit wants the body of Christ to know in these last days.

His Head and Hair

Daniel 7:9 KJV
I beheld till the thrones were cast down, and the Ancient of days did sit, whose garment was white as snow, and the hair of his head like the pure wool: his throne was like the fiery flame and his wheels as burning fire.

The Bible says in Revelation 1:14 that "His head and his hairs were white like wool, as white as snow". This correlates with the preceding scripture. When I see someone with white hair I think of old age, experience, longevity, etc. When I received this revelation, the Holy Spirit highlighted the Spirit of Wisdom to me. The white hair denotes wisdom. Isaiah 11:2 talks about the Spirit of wisdom and understanding, counsel and might, knowledge and the fear of the Lord. These all fall under the dimension of the Spirit of Wisdom. Throughout the Word of God wisdom, understanding, and knowledge are always connected or closely related. So when I read Isaiah 11:2 previously, I knew it wasn't totally correct but it wasn't totally incorrect either. The passage points us in the right direction but when we get there we still have to dig a bit deeper. Isaiah 11:2 reveals to us "one" of the seven Spirits of God, the Spirit of Wisdom.

The wisdom of God is not a commodity that mankind is inherently born with. The fear of the Lord is the beginning of wisdom (the wisdom of God) just as Jesus is wisdom's beginning. Wisdom must be sought after, found, and received. God in certain instances gave the spirit of wisdom to particular individuals.

> Exodus 28:3 KJV
> And thou shalt speak unto all that are wise hearted, whom I have filled with the spirit of wisdom, that they may make Aaron's garments to consecrate him, that he may minister unto me in the priest's office.

> Exodus 36:1 KJV
> Then wrought Bezaleel and Aholiab, and every wise hearted man, in whom the LORD put wisdom and understanding to know how to work all manner of work for the service of the sanctuary, according to all that the LORD had commanded.

In the New Testament we (the believer) can receive wisdom by simply asking for it (James 1:5). There are several types of wisdom; the wisdom of man or the world and the wisdom of God (James 3:15-18). There is also demonic wisdom, the wisdom of the forces of darkness.

Ephesians 1:16-17 KJV
Cease not to give thanks for you, making
mention of you in my prayers; That the God
of our Lord Jesus Christ, the Father of glory,
may give unto you the spirit of wisdom and
revelation in the knowledge of him:

Paul prayed that the Ephesian church would receive
the "spirit of wisdom and revelation", along with knowledge
and understanding. They had already received Jesus who
has been made unto us wisdom (1 Cor. 1:30) and the
Holy Spirit (the Spirit of Truth). But they still needed
the dimension of the Spirit of Wisdom to receive the full
revelation of Jesus Christ. We need to know who he is and
was, and what he has done for us and the place of power
he has brought us to. This applies to us today. We need
that revelation in order to walk in that power.

Wisdom is the principal thing just as Jesus Christ is
the most important one that we need.

Isaiah 11:2 mentions the six fold manifestation of the
Spirit of Wisdom. The Spirit of:

1. Wisdom (skill or reaching a point, place, or end
   result by doing it the right way)
2. Understanding (the ability to mentally separate in
   order to execute)
3. Counsel (advice or plan for deliverance or victory)
4. Might (great strength or authority, warrior, force,
   valor, victory and power)
5. Knowledge (to know or ascertain by seeing, we
   know that the Spirit knows all things even the

intents of our hearts. When I think of knowledge I also think of the knowledge of facts that are true).

6. The fear of the Lord (Awe or fear where one throws self at the mercy or feet of one in authority) (Heb. 10:31). It is the beginning of wisdom and knowledge (Prov. 1:7). It fears God and hates evil: pride, and arrogance, and the evil way, and the froward mouth, all the things God hates (Prov. 8:13). It hates what God hates.

Man was made in the image of God so he has the capacity to have his own wisdom. His wisdom comes through his experience in life. In the Old Testament it was to be passed down from generation to generation. But this doesn't guarantee wisdom to everyone. It must be desired and sought after and learned.

> Job 32:9 KJV
> Great men are not always wise: neither do
> the aged understand judgment.

We get the wisdom of God by asking for it. The Spirit of Wisdom is the avenue the Lord uses to infuse us with his wisdom.

His Eyes

Revelation 1:14 KJV
His head and his hairs were white like wool, as white as snow; and his eyes were as a flame of fire;

Jeremiah 5:3 KJV
3 O LORD, are not thine eyes upon the truth? …………

The next dimension is the Spirit of Truth. The Lord sees us through his eyes of truth. When I received the revelation that I am sharing with you, this one was probably the hardest to define. From what I can remember, the Holy Spirit saved it for last or one of the last, when he gave me the revelation. It was easier to get some of the others first before he gave me this one. There are so many lies that are before our eyes that the truth can be obscure to those who are not diligently seeking it. The scripture says "His eyes were as a flame of fire", God allows truth to be tested by fire. Truth will always prevail because God has ordained it to. Without truth, everything would fall apart.

I often look into a person's eyes to see if they are telling me the truth. I had to do this with one of my sons when he was about 4 or 5 years old. I could not tell when he was lying to me. I finally asked the Lord to show me when he was lying and he answered my prayer. There are some people who can lie and look you straight in the eye and you might believe them if you're not careful. There are also those who lie so well that they can fool a lie detector test. I believe this is why they are not admissible in court as evidence. Many of our politicians are these types of individuals. Many people including Christians chose to believe them anyway. You would think that Christians would know the truth when they hear it, but this is not always the case. My son at a young age was proficient at lying to me while looking me straight in the eyes. But the Holy Spirit helped me to tell when he was being untruthful. He helped me to break that bondage that was over him. The Holy Ghost is the Spirit of Truth. He cannot lie because he is truth.

> John 16:13 KJV
> Howbeit when he, the Spirit of truth, is come, he will guide you into all truth: for he shall not speak of himself; but whatsoever he shall hear, that shall he speak: and he will shew you things to come.

When Jesus comes back to catch up his church, he is going to judge the Body of Christ (every born again Christian believer). He will judge all God's children for their works. When he does this, I believe he is going to look on our works with his "fiery eyes of truth" and our works will be tried by fire. Some people may think that I am talking about working for our salvation. This not what I am saying, I am speaking about working for our reward. Take note of the following passage.

> 1 Corinthians 3:13-15 KJV
> Every man's work shall be made manifest: for the day shall declare it, because it shall be revealed by fire; and the fire shall try every man's work of what sort it is. If any man's work abide which he hath built thereupon, he shall receive a reward. If any man's work shall be burned, he shall suffer loss: but he himself shall be saved; yet so as by fire.

The apostle Paul is not talking about working for your salvation here; he is talking about working for your reward. I remember the first time I read this scripture; I began to think the Lord was letting people off the hook. In other words, I thought that he was going to allow people to be slack and they would then still be saved and go to heaven. The Spirit of Truth had to show me that the Word was not talking about sin in this passage, but that he was speaking of our work and the reward that we are going to receive when he comes back to catch up his church.

> Revelation 22:12 KJV
> And, behold, I come quickly; and my reward is with me, to give every man according as his work shall be.

I believe many people at that time are not going to receive any reward because they did not abide in or base their work in the truth. We will not be able to fake or perpetrate before the Lord when it comes to the nature of our work. It will be good or bad, valuable or worthless, or it may be some combination of the two extremes. Nevertheless the worthless works will be burned up and any precious works will remain.

> 1 Corinthians 3:11-12 KJV
> For other foundation can no man lay than that is laid, which is Jesus Christ. Now if any man build upon this foundation gold, silver, precious stones, wood, hay, stubble;

This is why we need the Spirit of Truth to guide us into all truth. If we don't walk in the truth when it comes to our work or ministry, we will not receive a reward or maybe even miss heaven all together. Gold, silver, precious stones, diamonds, cannot be destroyed by fire. They were created by fire, heat, and pressure and will only be purified by more heat, fire, and pressure. Wood, hay, and stubble will be completely burned up. If we fail to obey the Spirit of Truth we may lose all of our reward. The Holy Spirit is our comforter and he has been given to us to lead and guide us in our walk with the Lord. He was given to us to show us the way. Sin is very deceptive. It can sneak up on us and ensnare us if we are not careful. We must listen to the Spirit of Truth (the Holy Spirit) and learn to obey his every word. We must obey the Word of Truth and not our own desires and lusts.

Why do we need a comforter? We need the Spirit of truth because sin is deceitful, and the world is harsh. It's directly opposed to the things of God. And remember we have the tempter who is always trying to make us fall. We need the comforter to bring us back to our purpose.

In these last days the truth has been under attack. When I look at all the false teaching that is being proclaimed in the world today I don't have to guess why God would have to send the Spirit of Truth into the world. The Spirit of Truth keeps us focused and he helps us to discern the truth so that we won't go astray or be deceived by a false seducing spirit. Deception has a certain amount of truth in it; otherwise if it were an outright lie the person seeking some level of truth would not believe it. The Spirit of Truth has been given to us to guide us into all truth. We need to stay very close to the Holy Spirit who is the Spirit of Truth.

His Feet

Revelation 1:15 KJV
And his feet like unto fine brass, as if they burned in a furnace; and his voice as the sound of many waters.

Isaiah 4:4 KJV
When the Lord shall have washed away the filth of the daughters of Zion, and shall have purged the blood of Jerusalem from the midst thereof by the spirit of judgment, and by the spirit of burning.

The next dimension of the seven Spirits of God is the Spirit of Judgment. Brass is associated with the judgment of God. The Lord's feet are also mentioned in connection with the judgment of God. I used to think judgment was always bad until the Lord showed me otherwise. Judgment is negative for the sinner but positive for the believer. The passage says that he will "wash away the filth" and "purge the blood" by the spirit of judgment and the spirit of burning". This a positive move by God. He does this in order to cleanse us from our guilt and sin. The Spirit of Judgment is related to water baptism and to Holy Ghost baptism. Water baptism is a rite of purification, while Holy Spirit baptism is an infusion of purging and power. I believe the Spirit of Judgment facilitates this. God wants us free from our past sin and on fire for him. He wants to infuse us with his "firepower" against the works of the enemy. The Spirit of Judgment is involved in the purification and the power of the believer.

Judgment in the life of the child of God is very important. The Lord will judge us now if we do not judge ourselves. He does this so that we will not be judged with the world.

> 1 Corinthians 11:31-32, KJV
> For if we would judge ourselves, we should not be judged. But when we are judged, we are chastened of the Lord, that we should not be condemned with the world.

The Lord is concerned about our walk. He wants us to work in the kingdom but he also wants our walk to be correct.

> 1 Peter 4:17-18 KJV
> For the time is come that judgment must begin at the house of God: and if it first begin at us, what shall the end be of them that obey not the gospel of God? And if the righteous scarcely be saved, where shall the ungodly and the sinner appear?

This is why it is important for us to make sure we are walking upright before God. I believe that this is one of the reasons why we don't see more people operating in the power of God. If Satan can keep us in a mode of always feeling like our walk is not what it should be or if we always feel like we are or actually are under the judgment of God or close to it, we will most likely struggle with our confidence in God.

The Lord gives us the dimension of the Spirit of Judgment to help keep us from straying too far away from his holiness. Judgment is part of his redemptive process. It seems negative but it isn't, at least it is not negative to the born again Christian. Everything about God is positive even the things that seem like they are not. When the Holy Spirit deals with us about our sin, even though it seems negative, it is actually a positive thing because he is turning us around and bringing us back to himself (if we repent and turn our hearts in obedience towards him). I am not saying we should be living under the judgment of God all the time, but we should be living under "self" judgment and the fear of the Lord, which will cause us to avoid or miss the judgment of God.

Self-judgment also correlates with feet washing. Remember brass represents judgment. In the tabernacle the laver was a washbowl made of brass. I believe when they washed their hands and feet they were able to see themselves or see their reflection in the bottom of the laver.

> Exodus 30:17-21 KJV
> And the LORD spake unto Moses, saying,
> Thou shalt also make a laver of brass, and

his foot also of brass, to wash withal: and thou shalt put it between the tabernacle of the congregation and the altar, and thou shalt put water therein. For Aaron and his sons shall wash their hands and their feet thereat: When they go into the tabernacle of the congregation, they shall wash with water, that they die not; or when they come near to the altar to minister, to burn offering made by fire unto the LORD: So they shall wash their hands and their feet, that they die not: and it shall be a statute for ever to them, even to him and to his seed throughout their generations.

God wants his people and especially his leaders to keep themselves clean from the impurities of the world. He wants us to evaluate our walk and to also make sure that we also wash one another's feet. If we see another man or woman of God in ministry not walking right, we should pray about the situation and then confront them in love. A spirit of competition will keep leaders from washing each other's feet, practically and spiritually. This is a huge problem in the Body of Christ. I've found that in certain regions and cities, this spirit of competition among God's leaders is rampant. The Holy Spirit has already dealt with many leaders on this topic.

Feet washing exposes the fact that while we are walking in this world, we are exposed to the dirt that is in this world. We all need to wash the contamination of this world off of our feet, leaders and laity. In the next passage Jesus begins to wash the disciples' feet.

> John 13:5-10 AKJV
> After that he pours water into a basin, and began to wash the disciples' feet, and to wipe them with the towel with which he was girded. Then comes he to Simon Peter: and Peter said to him, Lord, do you wash my feet? Jesus answered and said to him, What I do you know not now; but you shall know hereafter. Peter said to him, You shall never wash my feet Jesus answered him, If I wash you not, you have no part with me. Simon Peter said to him, Lord, not my feet only, but also my hands and my head. Jesus said to him, he that is washed needs not save to wash his feet, but is clean every whit: and you are clean, but not all.

Notice in the passage Jesus said "he that is washed" or already washed. What he is saying here is this, the ones that were following him are already clean and only need to make sure that their feet are clean (except for Judas who was not clean), in other words, they need to make sure they walk in purity and in holiness. I believe he is saying that you have to be washed through the washing of regeneration first before you can qualify for feet washing (Titus 3:5). And if we are regenerated or born again and we don't allow our walk to be pure, we will have "no part with" him.

> John 3:36 KJV
> He that believeth on the Son hath everlasting life: and he that believeth not the Son shall not see life; but the wrath of God abideth on him.

The Bible speaks about the wrath of God. There will come a time when God will pour out his wrath upon this sinful world. I believe the Spirit of Judgment will facilitate this also. I don't want to be a recipient of God's punishment. But, in light of this, did you know that millions even billions of people are walking around with God's wrath abiding upon them. This is a sad and terrible thing and it is totally unnecessary. This is why Jesus died on the cross; to save sinners. And this is why we must preach the gospel to those who are lost, those who are not saved or born again.

> Matthew 12:18-21, KJV
> Behold my servant, whom I have chosen; my beloved, in whom my soul is well pleased: I will put my spirit upon him, and he shall shew judgment to the Gentiles. He shall not strive, nor cry; neither shall any man hear his voice in the streets. A bruised reed shall he not break, and smoking flax shall he not quench, till he

send forth judgment unto victory. And in
his name shall the Gentiles trust.

It has always been God's plan to bring salvation to
the non-Jew Gentile nations. Jesus touches on it the next
passage.

John 10:16, KJV
And other sheep I have, which are not of
this fold: them also I must bring, and they
shall hear my voice; and there shall be one
fold, [and] one shepherd.

Jesus is talking about the Gentile fold of sheep here.
This is us. The apostle Paul also mentions the oneness of
the two folds.

Ephesians 2:12-15, KJV
That at that time ye were without Christ,
being aliens from the commonwealth of
Israel, and strangers from the covenants
of promise, having no hope, and without
God in the world: But now in Christ
Jesus ye who sometimes were far off are
made nigh by the blood of Christ. For
he is our peace, who hath made both
one, and hath broken down the middle
wall of partition [between us]; Having
abolished in his flesh the enmity, [even]
the law of commandments [contained]

in ordinances; for to make in himself of
twain one new man, [so] making peace;

So as I mentioned earlier, the Spirit of Judgment can
be positive when it comes to the child of God but negative
to the unbeliever. The Spirit of Judgment can facilitate
much needed victory in our lives. Jesus bought victory to
us the Gentile nations and now through his grace and the
Spirit of Judgment, we are able to taste that victory.

His Voice

Revelation 1:15 KJV
And his feet like unto fine brass, as if they burned in a furnace; and his voice as the sound of many waters.

Ezekiel 43:2 KJV
And, behold, the glory of the God of Israel came from the way of the east: and his voice was like a noise of many waters: and the earth shined with his glory.

Revelation 21:6 KJV
And he said unto me, It is done. I am Alpha and Omega, the beginning and the end. I will give unto him that is athirst of the fountain of the water of life freely.

Revelation 11:11 KJV
And after three days and an half the Spirit of life from God entered into them, and they stood upon their feet; and great fear fell upon them which saw them.

The next dimension of the seven Spirits of God is the Spirit of Life. God is the God of the living (Mark 12:27). When the Holy Spirit revealed this dimension to me he easily caused me to see the connection between God's voice and the life of God. If you look at the progression in the preceding passages you can see a connecting truth. His voice is like the sound of many waters. Water is the key to life (our bodies are more than 60% water). And the Spirit of Life proceeds from God. When the Lord speaks he speaks life to us. When the devil speaks, he speaks death. When we speak, we can speak death or life. When we hear God's voice, we have a choice. We can choose to obey or choose to rebel. Adam chose to disobey and then hide. When we choose to submit to the voice of the Lord we choose everlasting life. When we refuse or rebel, we choose eternal death or damnation.

> John 4:14 KJV
> But whosoever drinketh of the water that I shall give him shall never thirst; but the water that I shall give him shall be in him a well of water springing up into everlasting life.

Everyone knows when we open our mouths to speak, we release moisture. I can't count how many times I breathed on a car window when I was a kid, in order to cause condensation so I could make a smiley face or write my name. When the Lord speaks, he releases waters in the earth's atmosphere.

Jeremiah 10:12-14 KJV
He hath made the earth by his power, he hath established the world by his wisdom, and hath stretched out the heavens by his discretion. When he uttereth his voice, there is a multitude of waters in the heavens, and he causeth the vapours to ascend from the ends of the earth; he maketh lightnings with rain, and bringeth forth the wind out of his treasures. Every man is brutish in his knowledge: every founder is confounded by the graven image: for his molten image is falsehood, and there is no breath in them.

When God created Adam, he breathed into him the breath of life and he became a living soul (Genesis 2:7). Breath is always associated with life. In order for us to live we must breathe. In order for us live spiritually we must receive and breathe in the life of God.

Matthew 4:4 KJV
But he answered and said, It is written, Man shall not live by bread alone, but by every word that proceedeth out of the mouth of God.

Jesus said "my sheep hear my voice and follow me". The child of God knows His voice because the child of God has chosen life.

John 10:24-28 KJV

Then came the Jews round about him, and said unto him, How long dost thou make us to doubt? If thou be the Christ, tell us plainly. Jesus answered them, I told you, and ye believed not: the works that I do in my Father's name, they bear witness of me. But ye believe not, because ye are not of my sheep, as I said unto you. My sheep hear my voice, and I know them, and they follow me: And I give unto them eternal life; and they shall never perish, neither shall any man pluck them out of my hand.

I used to know an anointed woman of God who used to say "to know Jesus is eternal life". I never forgot those anointed words because they are the truth. Jesus is the Word; he is the way, the truth, and the life. He is the Word of life (1 John 1:1).

Romans 8:1-2 KJV

There is therefore now no condemnation to them which are in Christ Jesus, who walk not after the flesh, but after the Spirit. For the law of the Spirit of life in Christ Jesus hath made me free from the law of sin and death.

The law of the Spirit of life in Christ Jesus supersedes the law of sin and death. The Spirit of Life is stronger than death. It is a liberating spirit, it is a bondage breaker. If a person is enslaved by the ravages of sin, the Spirit of Life will break those chains and set them free.

The Spirit of Life is also directly involved with the resurrection of the dead.

> Revelation 11:11, KJV
> And after three days and an half the Spirit of life from God entered into them, and they stood upon their feet; and great fear fell upon them which saw them.

Not one soul can or will be resurrected without the Spirit of Life.

His Hand

Revelation 1:16 KJV
And he had in his right hand seven
stars: and out of his mouth went a sharp
twoedged sword: and his countenance was
as the sun shineth in his strength.

Zechariah 12:10 KJV
And I will pour upon the house of David,
and upon the inhabitants of Jerusalem,
the spirit of grace and of supplications:
and they shall look upon me whom they
have pierced, and they shall mourn for
him, as one mourneth for his only son,
and shall be in bitterness for him, as one
that is in bitterness for his firstborn.

The next dimension of the seven Spirits of God is the
Spirit of Grace. The Lord had showed me in the past that
the number five is the number of grace. There is such a
thing as scriptural numerics and my heavenly Father is
the greatest mathematician. God does things according

to his own purpose and he uses numbers sometimes to accomplish whatever that purpose is. As we can see with the seven Spirits of God, the number "seven" is very important in scripture. It is God's complete number, or in other words, it is his number of perfection.

The number five is also significant in scripture. It is the number of grace. David had five smooth stones when he defeated Goliath (he only used one). Paul received thirty nine stripes five times. Jesus fed the five thousand. As you can see that the number five is significant.

Many have taught that grace is the unmerited favor of God, which is true. This is the favor of God that we have not worked for; all we had to do was receive and believe his word and begin to act on it. This grace or favor is something that we do not deserve, but he extends it to us anyway. We are not entitled to it and without it we cannot or will not ever stand in the presence of God.

For our purposes right now I am going to call this grace I'm speaking of the "general grace of God". We will see in the scriptures that often the grace of God is referred to in a general manner. The apostle Paul often wrote of God's grace by simply calling it "the grace of God"," the word of grace"," the gospel of grace" etc. If you look closely at the scriptures you will find that the Spirit of Grace manifests his power in multiple ways. There are actually five pillars of grace. The five pillars of grace are:

1. Saving grace (Eph. 1:7, 2:5-8)
2. Praying grace (Zech. 12:10, Heb. 4:16)
3. Enabling grace (Eph. 3:7, 4:7)

4. Great grace (Acts 4:33)
5. Providing grace (2 Cor. 8:9, 9:8)

I'm going to give you a quick overview of each one.

Frankly, this is why the grace of God is so important to us. We cannot be saved without the saving grace of God. The root word of the word grace in the Old Testament means to "to bend or stoop in kindness to an inferior". God the Father through Jesus Christ has extended his grace and mercy to us and saved us. The apostle Paul expounds on saving grace more than any of the others. It is so important because this is our way in to the salvation and blessings of God through Jesus Christ. There's no other way. That's why Jesus is the way. He is full of grace and truth.

In order for us to maintain a relationship with God he sent forth the Spirit of Grace to help us pray and supplicate before him. Isn't God awesome? He tells us to pray, and then he helps us in prayer. I'm not going to spend too much time here I will touch on prayer and its importance later on.

Then there is the "enabling favor of God". It is the ability to do whatever it is that God has called or ordained you to do. In Ephesians the fourth chapter the scripture mentions the fivefold ministry. These are five specific ministry gifts given to the Body of Christ to help us get to our preordained destiny.

I have understood one thing; in all the years I have been in ministry (28+ years), I could not have, or will not have, ever been able to do the work that the Lord has called me to do without the grace of God. This is that enabling grace or ability.

> 1 Timothy 1:12 KJV
> And I thank Christ Jesus our Lord, who hath enabled me, for that he counted me faithful, putting me into the ministry;

Jesus calls us and puts his anointing on our life and enables us to do the ministry that he has called us to. I am going to take it one step further; through us, Jesus is actually the apostle, the prophet, the evangelist, the pastor and the teacher (Ephesians 4:11). He works through us by the Spirit of Grace to accomplish his will as we yield to him.

"Great grace" manifests the power of God. We need to see more of the Spirit of Grace manifesting "great grace" in our midst. Miracles, signs and wonders are guaranteed to happen in this atmosphere. In the book of Acts great grace was manifested in the midst of the church led by the apostles.

Grace for provision and increase are also the work of the Spirit of Grace. If God has called us by his grace then he will provide by his grace. Our entire lives and ministry should be saturated with the grace of God by the Spirit of Grace. There is a process that must be followed though. Jesus gave us the blueprint. He is our foundation. I've learned that if we are not obedient we can short circuit our provision.

John saw in the hand of the angel of the Lord seven stars. What did the seven stars in his hand represent?

Revelation 1:20 KJV
The mystery of the seven stars which thou
sawest in my right hand, and the seven
golden candlesticks. The seven stars are
the angels of the seven churches: and the
seven candlesticks which thou sawest are
the seven churches.

The word "angel" in this verse can also be translated
"messenger". It is translated as messenger in reference to
John the Baptist in Mark 1:2. I believe Jesus is talking
about the leaders of these churches not actual angels. I
have come to this conclusion because of the language
that is used when the "messengers' are addressed in the
first three chapters of the Book of Revelation. God holds
his ministers/messengers in the right hand of his power.

1 Kings 18:46 KJV
And the hand of the LORD was on Elijah;
and he girded up his loins, and ran before
Ahab to the entrance of Jezreel.

Notice the hand of the Lord was on Elijah. The right
hand is associated with the power of God, in salvation
and deliverance.

Psalms 118:14-16 KJV
The LORD is my strength and song,
and is become my salvation. The voice
of rejoicing and salvation is in the
tabernacles of the righteous: the right

hand of the LORD doeth valiantly. The right hand of the LORD is exalted: the right hand of the LORD doeth valiantly.

Psalms 20:6 KJV
Now know I that the LORD saveth his anointed; he will hear him from his holy heaven with the saving strength of his right hand.

Psalms 89:13 KJV
Thou hast a mighty arm: strong is thy hand, and high is thy right hand.

The association of the number five and how it correlates with the hand of the Lord (with its five fingers) and the five pillars of grace is one of the reasons I believe that the Word of God is referring to the Spirit of Grace in Revelation 1:16.

His Mouth

Revelation 1:16 KJV
And he had in his right hand seven stars: and out of his mouth went a sharp twoedged sword: and his countenance was as the sun shineth in his strength.

Revelation 19:15 KJV
And out of his mouth goeth a sharp sword, that with it he should smite the nations: and he shall rule them with a rod of iron: and he treadeth the winepress of the fierceness and wrath of Almighty God.

Revelation 19:10 KJV
And I fell at his feet to worship him. And he said unto me, See thou do it not: I am thy fellowservant, and of thy brethren that have the testimony of Jesus: worship God: for the testimony of Jesus is the spirit of prophecy.

The next dimension of the seven Spirits of God is the Spirit of Prophecy. There is a difference between the Spirit of Prophecy and the Spirit of Life. They both proceed from the mouth and they both can bring life but, the Spirit of Prophecy can also bring death. It is militant to the extent that we cannot war with the spiritual forces of darkness without the Spirit of Prophecy.

> Matthew 8:16 KJV
> When the even was come, they brought unto him many that were possessed with devils: and he cast out the spirits with his word, and healed all that were sick:

Jesus shows us how the Spirit of Prophecy can be used to fight against our enemies. When we prophesy we are speaking a supernatural language in a known tongue. Prophecy is the Spirit of God speaking through us in words we can understand. Prophecy also speaks of and deals with future events where the Spirit of Life deals mostly with the present situation. I believe the Spirit of Prophecy and the Spirit of Life work together when a person is resurrected from the dead.

> Revelation 11:11-12 KJV
> And after three days and an half the Spirit of life from God entered into them, and they stood upon their feet; and great fear fell upon them which saw them. And they

heard a great voice from heaven saying unto them, Come up hither. And they ascended up to heaven in a cloud; and their enemies beheld them.

Hebrews 4:12 KJV
For the word of God is quick, and powerful, and sharper than any twoedged sword, piercing even to the dividing asunder of soul and spirit, and of the joints and marrow, and is a discerner of the thoughts and intents of the heart.

The testimony of Jesus Christ is the Spirit of Prophecy. Everything about prophecy is everything about Jesus. God wants us all to prophesy. The reason for this is that prophecy or prophesying also edifies and builds up the Body of Christ. Prophecy speaks life or death. The Lord wants us to understand that he wants us to put His words in our mouth and to limit our own words.

Numbers 11:29 KJV
And Moses said unto him, Enviest thou for my sake? would God that all the LORD'S people were prophets, and that the LORD would put his spirit upon them!

1 Corinthians 14:1 KJV
Follow after charity, and desire spiritual gifts, but rather that ye may prophesy.

1 Samuel 10:6 KJV
And the Spirit of the LORD will come upon thee, and thou shalt prophesy with them, and shalt be turned into another man.

When we prophesy we are speaking by the Spirit of God. When his Spirit comes upon a person that person should yield and say what the Lord wants them to say. Unfortunately it doesn't always happen that way because we have a free will and we can quench the Spirit if we want to. The end result of quenching the Spirit is not good. We also have to contend with our flesh, which gets in the way sometimes. And we need to know that we are yielding to the right spirit. In any event, we should always strive to be obedient to the Holy Spirit in every area of our lives including when it comes to prophesying.

1 Corinthians 14:32 KJV
And the spirits of the prophets are subject to the prophets.

The Spirit of Prophecy is very important in the kingdom of God. Many individuals choose to operate their ministries without yielding to the Spirit of Prophecy. You do not have be a prophet to prophesy. Anyone in the Body of Christ can prophesy. God can use a donkey to prophesy if he wants to. You are not someone who is better than everyone else if you allow God to use you to prophesy. But, when you do allow him to use you, you are building up the

Body of Christ and laying up a great reward for yourself in heaven.

There are those who are false prophets. So all prophecy should be judged. I remember there was a time when I was at a conference and the preacher was supposed to be prophesying to me but was actually not prophesying at all. He was trying to please the leadership of the conference I was attending (the Lord showed me this). He told me I was to move away to a certain town. I judged the prophetic word I had received and the Lord showed me he was off, and why he said what he said. I'm glad that I have a relationship with God and I hear from him. I believe in the Spirit of Prophecy. I believe in the prophetic word. I'm not afraid of it, but I also know that sometimes the spoken prophetic word is incorrect.

Like I said earlier, the Spirit of Prophecy is militant. When Jesus comes back he is going to speak and destroy his enemies.

> 2 Thessalonians 2:8, KJV
> And then shall that Wicked be revealed, whom the Lord shall consume with the spirit of his mouth, and shall destroy with the brightness of his coming:

> Revelation 19:15, KJV
> And out of his mouth goeth a sharp sword, that with it he should smite the nations: and he shall rule them with a rod of iron: and he treadeth the winepress of the fierceness and wrath of Almighty God.

Revelation 19:21, KJV
And the remnant were slain with the sword of him that sat upon the horse, which [sword] proceeded out of his mouth: and all the fowls were filled with their flesh.

This is the key to militant spiritual warfare. We need to learn how to use the sword of the Lord in our lives. The Word of God is that sword (Heb. 4:12).

His Countenance

Revelation 1:16 KJV
And he had in his right hand seven
stars: and out of his mouth went a sharp
twoedged sword: and his countenance was
as the sun shineth in his strength.

Numbers 6:24-26 KJV
The LORD bless thee, and keep thee: The
LORD make his face shine upon thee, and
be gracious unto thee: The LORD lift up
his countenance upon thee, and give thee
peace.

1 Peter 4:14 KJV
If ye be reproached for the name of Christ,
happy are ye; for the spirit of glory and of
God resteth upon you: on their part he
is evil spoken of, but on your part he is
glorified.

The final dimension of the seven Spirits of God is the
Spirit of Glory. God's ultimate aim is to be glorified in his

children. He has set up his whole redemptive plan in order to bring us into this place where we are glorifying him with great intensity. Our aim should be that we should always want God to get the glory in our lives. We should want Christ to be seen instead of ourselves.

> 1 Corinthians 6:18-20 KJV
> Flee fornication. Every sin that a man doeth is without the body; but he that committeth fornication sinneth against his own body. What? know ye not that your body is the temple of the Holy Ghost which is in you, which ye have of God, and ye are not your own? For ye are bought with a price: therefore glorify God in your body, and in your spirit, which are God's.

The enemy is constantly trying to get us to use our bodies, even our entire being, for everything else but for Gods purpose. God has commanded us to glorify him in our bodies. The world's aim is to do things that make them feel good; God's people should be aiming to do things to please God first. Remember the Lord is not trying to keep us from having fun but he is trying to keep us from destroying our lives, ourselves, and others. We need to do the things that are always pleasing to God. We belong to God and not to ourselves. When we do those things that God loves, our joy will always abound.

The Spirit of Glory manifests the tangible anointing of God. The root meaning of the word "glory" in the Old Testament is "to be heavy" in a good or bad sense.

> Psalms 8:4-5 KJV
> What is man, that thou art mindful of
> him? and the son of man, that thou visitest
> him? For thou hast made him a little lower
> than the angels, and hast crowned him
> with glory and honour.

God has also given mankind a limited type of glory because we were made in his image. Man's glory is also an outward manifestation of his material wealth and/ or possessions. Even then we are to give all of the glory unto God.

> Psalms 29:2 KJV
> Give unto the LORD the glory due unto
> his name; worship the LORD in the
> beauty of holiness.

When we live and walk in holiness we bring Glory to God.

Moses asked God to show him his glory (Exodus 33:18). The Lord told Moses he could not see his face or otherwise he would die. I believe Moses desired to see the Lord in this way because he wanted deeper intimacy with God. Ultimately, isn't this what all God's children should seek for? Shouldn't we seek a deep, intimate, relationship with the Lord? This is why Jesus died. This is one of the reasons why the seven Spirits of God have been sent into all the earth, to bring us into that deep personal relationship that God desires of us.

Ezekiel 43:5 KJV
So the spirit took me up, and brought
me into the inner court; and, behold, the
glory of the LORD filled the house.

There is so much more to this topic that I can't get
into at this time. But I encourage you to do a detailed study
on the glory of God from the glory of the tabernacle to the
glory of the Lord at his return.

One God, One Spirit, Seven Dimensions

Now that we have established the true revelation of the seven Spirits of God, which are as follows:

1. The Spirit of Grace
2. The Spirit of Judgment
3. The Spirit of Glory
4. The Spirit of Life
5. The Spirit of Prophecy
6. The Spirit of Truth
7. The Spirit of Wisdom

We now realize and know that the seven Spirits are the sevenfold dimension of the one Holy Spirit.

Unity vs Oneness

Ephesians 4:3-6 KJV
Endeavouring to keep the unity of the Spirit in the bond of peace. There is one body, and one Spirit, even as ye are called in one hope of your calling; One Lord, one faith, one baptism, One God and Father

> of all, who is above all, and through all,
> and in you all.

In the preceding passage (if we read it at face value) we may assume that the passage is stating that there is only "one" of everything in the list. But it is important to "rightly divide" or interpret the scripture here in order to get the big picture so that we do not misinterpret it as some have already done. Now, let's first look at the word "unity". The word unity in the passage simply means "oneness" as in the sense of being united, not one in number or one in the sense of being "single" or "alone". It means one as far as being together with one mind, one purpose, one destiny or goal, etc. With that in mind we can then see that the passages are focusing on unity and not focusing on singleness or the number of items in the list. For example, we know that there isn't only one physical body or person in the Body of Christ. The Body of Christ is the totality of all born again believers.

> 1 Corinthians 12:27 KJV
> Now ye are the body of Christ, and members in particular.

In fact there are actually millions, maybe even billions of actual physical bodies dead and alive; I have a body, you have body, he has a body, and she has a body. I know this may sound simple but it is actually beyond some peoples' thinking. Some people only see the letter of the Word and not the spirit of the Word.

1 Corinthians 12:12-14, KJV
For as the body is one, and hath many members, and all the members of that one body, being many, are one body: so also is Christ. For by one Spirit are we all baptized into one body, whether we be Jews or Gentiles, whether we be bond or free; and have been all made to drink into one Spirit. For the body is not one member, but many.

This passage is emphasizing the unity or oneness and the many members of the body united as one.

So, how does a person get into the body of Christ? The Lord Jesus said that a person must be born again.

John 3:6-7, KJV
That which is born of the flesh is flesh; and that which is born of the Spirit is spirit. Marvel not that I said unto thee, Ye must be born again.

When a person is born again, the Holy Spirit baptizes them into the body of Christ. There is a distinct difference between being baptized into the body by the Holy Ghost and being baptized with the Holy Spirit by Jesus. John the Baptist made this very clear.

Matthew 3:11, KJV
I indeed baptize you with water unto repentance: but he that cometh after me

is mightier than I, whose shoes I am not
worthy to bear: he shall baptize you with
the Holy Ghost, and [with] fire:

When a person is born again, the Holy Spirit
regenerates their human spirit. When this happens the
Father and the Son come to live in us. This then makes
us candidates to receive and be filled with the Holy Ghost.

John 14:23, KJV
Jesus answered and said unto him, If a
man love me, he will keep my words: and
my Father will love him, and we will come
unto him, and make our abode with him.

Water baptism represents our initial salvation
experience with God. The Father and the Son come to
live in us after we believe. When we believe we fall in love
with God and have a heart to obey his commandments.
After we believe and the Father and Son make their abode
in us. Jesus said he would send us the Comforter, the Spirit
of Truth, (who is the Holy Spirit) to us but we must have
already received the Father and the Son. Let's look at the
book of Romans and we will then get back to our main
point.

Romans 8:9, KJV
But ye are not in the flesh, but in the
Spirit, if so be that the Spirit of God dwell
in you. Now if any man have not the Spirit
of Christ, he is none of his.

Here we can clearly see that the apostle Paul mentions the Father and the Son when speaking about the initial salvation of the believer. I've mentioned these things in order to lay some foundation for my next points. If you can't understand this truth then you will have difficulty understanding the deep revelation in the remainder of this book. Now let's look at the phrase "one baptism". As we have already pointed out, there is more than one baptism mentioned in the scriptures. There is water baptism, there is the baptism of the believer into the body of Christ (1 Corinthians 12:13), and there is the baptism with the Holy Spirit. Hebrews the sixth chapter talks about multiple of "baptisms". When we baptize with water, we baptize one another. The Holy Spirit baptizes us into the body of Christ. Jesus baptizes us with the Holy Spirit. There are three distinct baptisms mentioned here. There are others mentioned in the Bible also. Note the plurality or multiple baptisms mentioned in the following passage.

> Hebrews 6:1-2 KJV
> Therefore leaving the principles of the doctrine of Christ, let us go on unto perfection; not laying again the foundation of repentance from dead works, and of faith toward God, Of the doctrine of baptisms, and of laying on of hands, and of resurrection of the dead, and of eternal judgment.

So why is the apostle Paul listing all of the items in Ephesians 4:3-6 as one? Again, he is emphasizing the unity of the Spirit. So we can see that the Bible does not say in the scriptures that all the items in the list are exclusively "one" in number. This brings us to the point that I want to get across. Ephesians 4:4 does not contradict the references to the seven Spirits of God throughout the rest of scripture. So, as we can see the sevenfold dimension of the Holy Spirit is not limited to one single manifestation of the Spirit. To make myself clear I am talking about the mention of "one Spirit" in the book of Ephesians and "seven Spirits of God" in the book of Revelation. There is a sevenfold dimension of the (one) Holy Spirit which is rooted in how and when he (the Holy Spirit) was sent into the world. Ephesians chapter four does emphasize unity in the Body of Christ. It does not say that the Holy Spirit is only capable of functioning as one individual spirit, accomplishing one thing at a time. God is omnipresent (present everywhere at the same time); he does this through the Holy Spirit.

One God

In the passage "one God" is mentioned. The scripture is clear about God the Father being "one" God. But even when you look at the passage in Ephesians, you see clearly there are the Spirit, the Son, and the Father ("one Lord" is making reference to Jesus, the Son). So what does the Bible mean when it says that there is only "one God"? The Father, Son, and Holy Spirit are all one in nature and essence, one mind, one purpose, one goal or destiny, and one in spirit, etc. In Ephesians chapter 4 we see "one Spirit", "one Lord", and "one God". Often in the Word of

God you will see that Jesus is referred to as "Lord" and many times when the word "God" is used, the Bible is making reference to God the Father. It's not exclusively patterned this way throughout scripture but in certain passages you can see a distinct pattern. When the Scripture says there is only "one God", it is not excluding Jesus the Son but acknowledging the Father's supreme authority as the most high God, King, and creator of the universe. 1 Corinthians 8:6 reveals this point.

> 1 Corinthians 8:4-6, KJV
> As concerning therefore the eating of those things that are offered in sacrifice unto idols, we know that an idol is nothing in the world, and that there is none other God but one. For though there be that are called gods, whether in heaven or in earth, (as there be gods many, and lords many,) But to us there is but one God, the Father, of whom are all things, and we in him; and one Lord Jesus Christ, by whom are all things, and we by him.

The Bible says he is "One God and Father of all, who is above all, and through all, and in you all" (Eph. 4:4). And more specifically, the Father, Son and Holy Spirit were all involved in creation.

Take note of the words in the preceding passage "we by him". We were created "by" him. We were created by whom? The Son, the Lord Jesus Christ. This scripture shows a clear distinction between the Father and the Son.

This distinction is all throughout the Word of God. It is hard to miss. There are many, many examples that I could use in the Word to prove this point. And yet we know that the Father and Son are one.

> 1 Timothy 2:5 KJV
> For there is one God, and one mediator between God and men, the man Christ Jesus;

The children of Israel were surrounded by and exposed to nations and people that worshiped multiple gods. God wanted them to know and demonstrate that there is only one God and he alone exists and he is the one who created them. The Son proceeds from the Father, and the Holy Spirit proceeds from the Father as well.

> Mark 12:28-32 KJV
> And one of the scribes came, and having heard them reasoning together, and perceiving that he had answered them well, asked him, Which is the first commandment of all? And Jesus answered him, The first of all the commandments is, Hear, O Israel; The Lord our God is one Lord: And thou shalt love the Lord thy God with all thy heart, and with all thy soul, and with all thy mind, and with all thy strength: this is the first commandment. And the second is like, namely this, Thou shalt love thy neighbour as thyself. There

> is none other commandment greater than
> these. And the scribe said unto him, Well,
> Master, thou hast said the truth: for there
> is one God; and there is none other but he:

The word "one" used in this passage in the Old Testament is translated as the word united. This confirms my point and gives us a bit more insight. Also the word "God" is the word Elohim which is a pluralistic word.

Let's breakdown the oneness of God; God is self-existent and eternal. He has always existed. He has no beginning or does not have an end. Jesus is the Word of God and he has always existed and has no beginning as well as the Father. He was and has always been in the Father. Did you ever practically think about how Jesus as the Word relates to the Father? Now, I want you to take the limits off your thoughts of God and not confine him to mankind's finite existence. Think about this, when the world was created God spoke the Word. And the Word executed the work and created whatever he spoke. Jesus is God because he is his Word. He is Creator because he is his Word. He was not a created being because he has always been in God the Father and with God the Father. He is self-existent and eternal just as the Father is. Now, when a human speaks, his words have power. When we speak we can speak life or death. Jesus is the personification of God's power. This is where we stumble because Jesus is God's Word but our words are not a distinct separate person from us. But that is what the Lord is. He is the very essence of God personified. So he is God. Now, if you understand what I just laid out for you, we can apply the same principle to the Holy Spirit. Except, that the Holy Spirit was sent forth (just as Jesus was) but he is omnipresent as he was sent forth into the entire world. Jesus was not omnipresent because he had to take the form of a man in order to go to the cross and shed his blood and die for us. But through the Holy Spirit he is omnipresent because they are one. But remember the Spirit of Truth could not come until he left (John 16:7). The Holy Ghost is manifest in his sevenfold dimension and facilitates Gods will in the earth. He is the very essence of God. He is his inner being and he is able to fill all things. This is why the Bible says the Father fills all things. Jesus is subordinate to the Father and the Holy Spirit is subordinate to both the Father and the Son (Jesus). Jesus and the Holy Spirit are both submissive to the Father because they proceed from the Father. But yet they are equally God. This is why the Bible consistently says there is one God. And yet he is manifested in three persons.

> 1 John 5:7, KJV
> For there are three that bear record in heaven, the Father, the Word, and the Holy Ghost: and these three are one.

Jesus is not a separate God. The Holy Spirit is not a separate God. The scripture does not advocate three gods. Just as we have a human spirit God has his Spirit. Just as we communicate with words God has his Word (Jesus). Our words originate from our hearts. Jesus is the heart of God the Father personified. And yet he sent his own Spirit and his Word (his son and his heart) to us. The Lord Jesus is subordinate to the Father but he is also equal with the Father.

The children of Israel did not see a full revelation of Jesus. But we do know that they thought that if a man called himself a "son" he was putting himself on the same level as his father. This is why they wanted to stone Jesus when he called God his father. Notice that the Lord did not dispute the belief that he was making himself equal with God by saying he was his son.

> John 5:18 AKJV
> Therefore the Jews sought the more to kill him, because he not only had broken the sabbath, but said also that God was his Father, making himself equal with God.

> Philippians 2:6-8, KJV
> Who, being in the form of God, thought it not robbery to be equal with God: But made himself of no reputation, and took upon him the form of a servant, and was made in the likeness of men: And being found in fashion as a man, he humbled himself, and became obedient unto death, even the death of the cross.

We now know, since the plan of salvation has been revealed, that Jesus is God. Emmanuel means "God with us". But he is God in the sense that he is the very nature, essence and express image of God the Father. Not in the sense that he and the Father are one in the same individual. It is clear that the Father and Son are not the same personification. Otherwise why would the following scripture say that Jesus is God's "express image of his person?" That denotes that they are separate individuals.

> Hebrews 1:1-3 KJV
> God, who at sundry times and in divers manners spake in time past unto the fathers by the prophets, Hath in these last days spoken unto us by his Son, whom he hath appointed heir of all things, by whom also he made the worlds; Who being the brightness of his glory, and the express image of his person, and upholding all things by the word of his power, when he had by himself purged our sins, sat down on the right hand of the Majesty on high;

How can Jesus sit down on the Father's right hand if they are the same individual? We know that Jesus looks just like our heavenly Father because he said "if you have seen me you have seen the Father".

> John 14:9 KJV
> Jesus saith unto him, Have I been so long time with you, and yet hast thou not known me, Philip? he that hath seen me hath seen the Father; and how sayest thou then, Shew us the Father?

As I reiterated earlier, the Father, Son, and Holy Spirit are one in nature but separate in individuality, function, and work. They are one in spirit and in essence with the same mind, purpose, and goal or destiny. But they do not do the exact same work or have the same function, nor are they the same persons or individuals. They work together within the interconnected framework of duty. Yet, they work together towards the same purposes. But they proceed from the same essence because they are one.

> 1 Corinthians 12:4-6 KJV
> Now there are diversities of gifts, but the same Spirit. And there are differences of administrations, but the same Lord. And there are diversities of operations, but it is the same God which worketh all in all.

If the Father, Son, and Holy Spirit were limited as being the same individual, then God would clearly state that in his Word and whenever he appeared, he would show up that way. Of course God can do whatever he wants to do and it would be okay because he is God. But, he constrains himself to his Word of truth (Psalms 138:2). So, if he represents himself as something other than what he is, he would be presenting himself as a liar and he cannot lie. He is Truth and he cannot act contrary to his own nature.

Jesus said himself that the Comforter (which is the Holy Spirit) could not come until he leaves.

> John 16:7 AKJV
> Nevertheless I tell you the truth; It is expedient for you that I go away: for if I go

not away, the Comforter will not come to
you; but if I depart, I will send him to you.

This obviously shows us that the Lord Jesus and the
Holy Spirit are separate individuals but also one. The Holy
Spirit is the only tangible connection on earth we have
with the Father and the Son. We have angels that minister
to us, but the Holy Ghost moves in and abides in and with
us. He causes us to walk in God's will. At the baptism of
Jesus, God the Father and the Holy Spirit showed up (Matt
3:16-17). In the book of Genesis God said "let US make
man" (Gen 1:27). He wasn't speaking to the angels because
the angels are created beings themselves. The Father, Son
and Holy Ghost took part in all of creation, so he was
talking to the Lord Jesus and the Holy Spirit of God when
he created mankind.

Why did we have to dive into all of this? Because in
order to fully understand this teaching about the seven
Spirits of God we must understand that the Holy Spirit
is one Spirit, but can function simultaneously in several
different modes or dimensions. His dimension is sevenfold.
I wanted to show you that the foundation of God's purpose
in his redemptive plan is based on unity and the plurality
of function, work and action. And with this, the work is
always accomplished with a full supply of the power of the
Holy Ghost. Which makes the power of the Spirit always
available at all times to everyone who believes.

Sometimes when I look at how some born again
Christians are responding to the things of God I can see
how one would get the impression that God is shorthanded

or that he doesn't have power. But that is not the case. All the power of heaven is available to the person that believes and acts on His Word. Jesus wears many hats and he never comes up short because of the sufficiency of the sevenfold dimension of the Spirit.

> Philippians 1:19 KJV
> For I know that this shall turn to my salvation through your prayer, and the supply of the Spirit of Jesus Christ,

We need a true revelation of what is available to us in the Spirit and how to tap into the power of God for us today (Eph. 1:18-19). The Bible says that he has given us all things that pertain to life and godliness (2 Peter 1:3).

We need to know and understand that in every situation we are empowered to triumph by the sevenfold manifestation of the Holy Ghost. The Holy Spirit is the divine dynamic power that powers this redemptive machine that God has sent into all the earth.

The Rainbow Light around His Throne

Revelation 4:2-3 KJV
And immediately I was in the spirit: and, behold, a throne was set in heaven, and one sat on the throne. And he that sat was to look upon like a jasper and a sardine stone: and there was a rainbow round about the throne, in sight like unto an emerald.

Let There Be Light

In Genesis chapter one, we read the account of how God created the heaven and the earth. Then, the very next thing he did was create light. What would be the first thing you would do if you were getting ready to begin a big project that had many intricate details and tasks? The first thing I would do is turn on the "light". I would find the best light I had available. That's what God did when he created the heaven and the planet earth, he turned on the light.

Genesis 1:3-5 KJV

And God said, Let there be light: and
there was light. And God saw the light,
that it was good: and God divided the
light from the darkness. And God called
the light Day, and the darkness he called
Night. And the evening and the morning
were the first day.

Remember God is not limited to a narrow visible
spectrum as we humans are. He did not need a source of
visible light to see. If you look at the following verses you
will see that God did not create the sun, moon, and the
stars until the fourth day.

Genesis 1:14-19 KJV

And God said, Let there be lights in the
firmament of the heaven to divide the day
from the night; and let them be for signs,
and for seasons, and for days, and years: And
let them be for lights in the firmament of the
heaven to give light upon the earth: and it
was so. And God made two great lights; the
greater light to rule the day, and the lesser
light to rule the night: he made the stars also.
And God set them in the firmament of the
heaven to give light upon the earth, And to
rule over the day and over the night, and to
divide the light from the darkness: and God
saw that it was good. And the evening and
the morning were the fourth day.

So why does scripture say the Lord God created "light" before he created the sun, moon, and the stars. I believe the reason why God created light on the first day and the sun, moon, and the stars on the fourth day is this; when he created light on the first day, he created what we now call the "electromagnetic spectrum (EMS)" first. The EMS is the entire wavelength spectrum including wavelengths we cannot see, and the visible wavelengths we can see. Of course God can see the invisible wavelengths we cannot see, as I mentioned before. The EMS includes radio waves, microwaves, infrared radiation, the visible waves or spectrum, ultraviolet radiation, x-rays, and gamma rays. The visible spectrum is the light we can see with our human eye. If he had not created the electromagnetic spectrum first, we would not have been able to see any other light in the visible spectrum that was created afterward. The human eye is a masterpiece of creation, but God purposely created our eyes with a visible limitation. There are animals that can see at night in darkness much better than humans can see. This is evident of the fact that even without sunlight or in total darkness they still have some other type of light. Just because humans can't see it naturally (that light), doesn't mean it does not exist. We don't need sunlight to have light. We have found out how to create a light source without the light from the sun. I didn't say we do not need the sun, I said we don't need the sun to have light. The sun is the best type of natural light. God created light (the EMS) before he created sun. Without it, we would not have been able to see the sun, moon or the stars.

The Rainbow and the Seven Spirits

White light in the visible spectrum consists of light which is the combination of all the colors of the rainbow. When a rainbow is visible, we are seeing the seven different components or colors of the white light separated. This also happens when we shine light though a prism. This process is called refraction. Raindrops cause light to refract at certain angles. God caused this phenomenon to happen after the flood when he made his covenant with Noah.

> Genesis 9:12-14 KJV
> And God said, This is the token of the covenant which I make between me and you and every living creature that is with you, for perpetual generations: I do set my bow in the cloud, and it shall be for a token of a covenant between me and the earth. And it shall come to pass, when I bring a cloud over the earth, that the bow shall be seen in the cloud:

There has been a difference of opinion among scientists, as to whether there are six or seven colors of light in the visible rainbow. The color "indigo" is the color they disagree about as to whether it should be included or not. I believe there are seven colors which include the color "indigo" simply because the number "seven" lines up perfectly with the seven Spirits of God.

The seven colors of the rainbow are seen in the visible spectrum in this order:

1. Red
2. Orange
3. Yellow
4. Green
5. Blue (sky blue)
6. Indigo (dark blue)
7. Violet (purple)

ROYGBIV, we all remember that from our school days, right? Do you know that the seven Spirits of God line up with the seven colors of the rainbow? Here is what the Spirit of Truth revealed to me early one morning while I was meditating on the Word of God.

1. Red = The Spirit of Grace
    a. The color red either stirs up hate and anger or it speaks of compassion, favor, mercy and forgiveness. If a wild carnivore smells or sees blood (a bear can smell blood from miles away) it will go into hunt and attack mode. When God sees blood, it stirs his mercy, compassion, grace and forgiveness, unless it is the result of his judgment.
    b. With God, if you are in the blood bought camp, you will receive grace, mercy, compassion, and forgiveness. But, if you are outside the camp you will receive damnation.
    c. There are those that shed blood and those that want to prevent the shedding of blood and/or stop the bleeding.

d. The blood of Jesus frees us from, and takes away our sins, sanctifies, and separates us from the world. This is positional sanctification carried out by the Spirit of Grace (1 John 1:7).

e. The Spirit of Grace is connected to and facilitates faith, prayer, power, and the gifts of the Spirit.

f. We enter into God's holy and sacred place by the (red) blood of Jesus (Hebrews 10:19).

2. Orange (brass or bronze) = The Spirit of Judgment

a. Orange is the color of fire which depicts God's fiery judgment. To the sinner judgment is a bad thing; to the believer it brings cleansing, purification and deliverance.

b. Baptism is linked to the Spirit of Judgment; water baptism and Holy Ghost fire baptism.

3. Yellow (gold) = The Spirit of Glory

a. Just as gold is precious in the earth, God's glory is precious and valuable in the kingdom of heaven.

b. Man thinks his gold is his glory. God's glory is his gold.

c. God's anointing oil is also gold in color (olive oil).

d. The glory of the Lord and that which produces it is more precious than all the gold in the world.

e. Yellow is also associated with the sun which is associated with the glory of the Lord (Rev 1:16).

f. The materialistic spirit loves gold more than it loves God. God hates the materialistic spirit.

It was that same spirit that Judas had when he betrayed Jesus. Judas sold out the Lord for 30 pieces of silver. And yet, God used Judas to accomplish his purpose.

4. Green = The Spirit of Life
   a. Who doesn't know that green speaks of life? Spring is green but it also speaks of the resurrection of life. Spiritual and physical resurrection.
   b. Green is the color of abundant flourishing prosperity. It speaks of fertility and growth. Green has a calming effect. It is the color which represents full provision and sufficiency.

5. Blue = The Spirit of Prophecy
   a. We have Prophetic Spoken Authority.
   b. We use our spoken words to take authority over the enemy.
   c. The heavens are blue. Blue is the color of a prophetic Word from the "blue" heaven.
   d. We have authority over the prince of the power of the air, spiritual wickedness in high places because our enemy abides in the high places of the (blue) heavens.

6. Indigo (dark blue) = The Spirit of Truth
   a. Sometimes indigo is hard to see or distinguish from blue or some shades of purple, just as "truth" is hard to see at times. We must diligently take care to rightly divide the truth.
   b. Indigo is the color in the rainbow or the visible spectrum that some in the world cannot or do not want to see or acknowledge. This points

to how there are many who don't want to, or can't see the truth of God's Word.

   c.   Indigo is also a color of authority which points to the authority of God's Word of truth. Notice that many authority figures use some shade of dark blue in their uniform.

7.   Purple (violet) = The Spirit of Wisdom

   a.   This is majestic kingly authority. The Spirit of wisdom is majestic royalty. Kings are expected to be wise (King Solomon).

   b.   The Spirit of Wisdom is manifested in spiritual warfare.

   c.   Purple has the most energy in the visible spectrum which points to its correlation with kingly authority and power.

Now I would like to get a little deeper into the color "indigo" or blue. When God told the children of Israel to make Aaron's holy garments, he told them to make the hem of the garment with embroidered pomegranates of blue, purple and scarlet (Exodus 28:33). He later told them to make fringes on the hem of their garments in the color blue which represented his holy commandments (Num. 15:38). After diligent study, research, and the revelation of the Spirit, I believe the blue in this passage is the color "indigo" which is a dark blue between the colors (sky) blue and violet (purple) in the visual color spectrum. Indigo is the color represented by the Spirit of Truth. When they looked at the color (blue) indigo they would remember his truth. This is significant because we can now clearly see the correlation between truth and the color "blue" mentioned in the Old Testament. To add to this let's take note of one important point. The word "blue" in the Old Testament is translated from the Hebrew word "tkeleth". This is the name used for the blue dye that is extracted from a snail found in the northern coasts of Israel. This snail produces both blue and purple dye. This is the reason the King James Version sometimes translates it as "purple". The blue dye can only be produced when the dye is exposed to ultraviolet light from the sun. This is the dye that was used to make the blue fabric that God commanded the Israelites to use when they made the hems of the garments for the priest, the veil that was in the temple and the fringes on the edges of their garments. When they looked on this color they were to remember the commandments of the Lord or remember his truth. God wanted the children of Israel to always remember his truth.

Photosynthesis in Creation

Another miracle and evidence of God's handy work in creation is the process of what is called "photosynthesis". It is the process that plants and other organisms use to capture light energy from the sun and convert it to chemical energy that can be burned for fuel. When we look at the sun we can see that it is mostly yellow. After the sunlight gets past the ozone layer the green plants absorb the remaining light. They don't absorb all of it though. Scientist say it reflects back almost half of the green and yellow colors and it absorbs mostly all of the blue and red colors. The reflection is what makes the plant green in color.

This is what the Holy Spirit showed me concerning the handy work of God's creative power. Color is measured in nanometers (nm). If you look at the nanometer numbers of the colors that a green plant absorbs, you will see that scientists say it absorbs in the range of 445 nm (blue light) and 670 nm (red light) the most. Remember when I mentioned that some scientists don't recognize indigo in the visible color spectrum. Indigo's nanometer range is between 420 and 450. The nanometer number 445 falls right within this range. Here is an example of the awesome work of God's creation. As I noted before indigo's visible color blue represents the Spirit of Truth and the color red represents the Spirit of Grace. What does the Bible say about Grace and Truth?

> John 1:4 KJV
> In him was life; and the life was the light
> of men. And the light shineth in darkness;
> and the darkness comprehended it not.

Look at what the Word says next within the same context of scripture.

> John 1:14 KJV
> And the Word was made flesh, and dwelt
> among us, (and we beheld his glory, the
> glory as of the only begotten of the Father,)
> full of grace and truth.

Praise God! I almost jumped out of my seat when I saw this. The two colors that natural plants absorb the most are the two colors that represent Grace and Truth. We are under Grace and Truth we are no longer under the law. Jesus made this happen.

> John 1:17 KJV
> For the law was given by Moses, but grace
> and truth came by Jesus Christ.

Jesus shines the light of Grace and Truth on us and into our hearts. Grace and Truth are the very things we need in these last days to grow and be whatever it is that God has predestined us to be.

Notice red and indigo are absorbed more than any other color by the green plant. Green represents the Spirit of Life. In order to truly live we must walk continually in his Grace and Truth.

> John 9:5 KJV
> As long as I am in the world, I am the
> light of the world.

> John 8:12 KJV
> Then spake Jesus again unto them,
> saying, I am the light of the world: he that
> followeth me shall not walk in darkness,
> but shall have the light of life.

Jesus is the light of the world. He has the seven Spirits of God without measure. He shines with a sevenfold manifestation of the Spirit. Just as white light has its seven spectrums of colors Jesus has the seven Spirits of God.

The fact that the church is in Christ and that Christ is in the church makes the church the light of the world also.

> Matthew 5:14-16 KJV
> Ye are the light of the world. A city that is set on an hill cannot be hid. Neither do men light a candle, and put it under a bushel, but on a candlestick; and it giveth light unto all that are in the house. Let your light so shine before men, that they may see your good works, and glorify your Father which is in heaven.

The Word, the Spirit, and the Principal of Duality

Ephesians 1:13 KJV
In whom ye also trusted, after that ye heard the word of truth, the gospel of your salvation: in whom also after that ye believed, ye were sealed with that holy Spirit of promise,

The Two Witnesses

Shortly after the Lord revealed the seven Spirits of God to me, he also began to show me additional revelation concerning another mystery in the scriptures, specifically in the Book of Revelation. It was the mystery of the two witnesses in Revelations chapter 11. Actually this topic should not qualify as a mystery at all, simply because it is plainly revealed in the scriptures if we would trust the Spirit of Wisdom to show us how to interpret the truth that he has given us. He showed me a connection between the seven Spirits of God, the two witnesses, and his principle of duality.

Revelation 11:3-6 KJV
And I will give power unto my two witnesses,
and they shall prophesy a thousand two
hundred and threescore days, clothed in
sackcloth. These are the two olive trees,
and the two candlesticks standing before
the God of the earth. And if any man will
hurt them, fire proceedeth out of their
mouth, and devoureth their enemies: and
if any man will hurt them, he must in this
manner be killed. These have power to shut
heaven, that it rain not in the days of their
prophecy: and have power over waters to
turn them to blood, and to smite the earth
with all plagues, as often as they will.

Over the years, I noticed that the identity of the two
witnesses seemed to be a topic of great debate. I had,
along with others, come to the conclusion that the two
witnesses are Moses and Elijah. But later on the Spirit of
God confirmed that conclusion in my spirit. I saw that
the choice of Elijah seems to be okay with many, but the
choice of Moses seems to be a heated controversy. I didn't
see a problem with Moses as one of the two witnesses. The
reason I came to this conclusion was the fact I had also
read in the gospels that Moses and Elijah appeared with
Jesus at his transfiguration.

Luke 9:28-30 KJV
And it came to pass (about) eight days
after these sayings, he took Peter and John

and James, and went up into a mountain
to pray. And as he prayed, the fashion
of his countenance was altered, and his
raiment was white and glistering. And,
behold, there talked with him two men,
which were Moses and Elias:

Just a side note here, as you can see in this scripture,
the Lord manifested his glory or you can say that the
seven Spirits of God manifested through the Lord's face
and garments. Remember as we saw in the last chapter
that white light is created from the combination of all the
colors in the visible rainbow.

"Elias" is how Elijah's name is spelled in the New
Testament. In spite of this scripture, there are still those
that don't think Moses is one of the two witnesses. Their
choice is Enoch instead of Moses. If this is correct, then
why wasn't Enoch at the mount of transfiguration with Jesus
instead of Moses? This is one of the reasons I disagree with
the choice of Enoch, and also because of what the Holy
Spirit has revealed to me concerning this topic. Enoch is a
type of the New Testament, New Covenant believer that
will be alive when Jesus comes back for the church at the
rapture. I believe that when I show the details of what the
Holy Spirit has revealed to me that there will be no question
as to whether the two witnesses are Moses and Elijah.

The Principle of Duality

God chooses to do things often from a dualistic frame of
reference. As I mentioned earlier he works with a "principle

of duality". When he created the universe he even used this dualistic approach. There are many things in our lives that we haven't thought about that are dualistic in nature. He used this dualism when he created light. I explained in the previous chapter that two of the seven colors of the rainbow that green plants absorb the most are Indigo (dark blue) and Red. Indigo and Red represent the Spirit of Truth (indigo) and the Spirit Grace (red). There is also another dualism that our Creator has used. You will find this if you observe how light behaves.

There was a debate for many years as to whether light was a wave, or was it a combination of particles. Eventually scientists came to the conclusion that it consisted of both. At that point the theory of "wave-particle duality" was embraced. Today, physicists accept the dual nature of light. This is what God knew all the time. He is the one that created it that way and he also created components in the spiritual realm with the same dualistic frame of reference. When "white" light is seen it is a combination of all the seven colors of the rainbow, but as it travels at the speed of light, it behaves in a dualistic manner as waves and particles. The Holy Spirit revealed to me that this dualism represents the Word of God and the Spirit of God. Jesus said he is the "light of the world" (John 9:5), and he is also the Word of God (John 1:1). The Holy Spirit is represented in scripture as olive oil. This is the same oil that is used to light the candlesticks in the temple and the lamps of the five wise virgins (Matt. 25 1-13).

Moses, Elijah, and Enoch

The reason I believe Moses and Elijah are the two witnesses is because they represent God's dualistic work. Moses represents the Law and Elijah represents the Prophets.

> Romans 3:21 KJV
> But now the righteousness of God without
> the law is manifested, being witnessed by
> the law and the prophets;

The law and the prophets are also witnesses. If you look again you can see that the Law represents the Word of God and the Prophets represents the Spirit of God. Take note of the following dualistic comparisons:

- The Word and the Spirit
- The Law and the Prophets
- Moses and Elijah
- Grace and Truth
- Bible Study and Prayer
- Jesus' Body and His Blood
- Prayer and Fasting
- Food and Drink
- Solid and Liquid

Another reason I also believe that the two witnesses are Moses and Elijah is the power that they will have. They have both displayed these powers in the past.

Revelation 11:6 KJV
These have power to shut heaven, that it rain not in the days of their prophecy: and have power over waters to turn them to blood, and to smite the earth with all plagues, as often as they will.

Elijah prayed that it would not rain and it didn't rain for three and a half years.

James 5:17-18 KJV
Elias was a man subject to like passions as we are, and he prayed earnestly that it might not rain: and it rained not on the earth by the space of three years and six months. And he prayed again, and the heaven gave rain, and the earth brought forth her fruit.

Moses turned the rivers to blood in Egypt when God sent him to free his people.

Exodus 7:20 KJV
And Moses and Aaron did so, as the LORD commanded; and he lifted up the rod, and smote the waters that were in the river, in the sight of Pharaoh, and in the sight of his servants; and all the waters that were in the river were turned to blood.

Moses also "smote" Egypt with all sorts of plagues. Moses has more evidence pointing to the fact that he is one of the two witnesses than Enoch does. Some say, the fact that Enoch was translated and never died and Elijah was translated and never died proves that Enoch is one of the two witnesses mentioned in the scriptures. But Enoch did not write a good portion of the Old Testament (which is the Word of God) by the inspiration of the Holy Spirit as Moses did. Neither has he done any of the miracles mentioned in Revelation 11:6. And besides this, the scripture says that Moses' body was taken by Michael the archangel. There is no one else in the Bible (that I know of) that has had their body "physically" taken at death in the same manner, (by an angel) as Moses has had his body taken.

> Jude 1:9 KJV
> Yet Michael the archangel, when contending with the devil he disputed about the body of Moses, durst not bring against him a railing accusation, but said, The Lord rebuke thee.

Actually God himself buried Moses (Deut. 34:5-6). The scripture said that no man knew where Moses' body was buried. This is probably when the dispute happened (or it happened sometime before or after this). Michael was most likely commanded to take Moses' body and the devil protested but could not stop him. I believe God did this because he knows he is going to bring Moses back during the seven year tribulation period along with Elijah.

Moses actually died. At the time of Moses' death, Satan had the keys to death and hell. This is why he disputed with the archangel Michael over Moses' body; he felt he had a right to the body of Moses. But remember Jesus has the keys now and God has the final authority (Rev. 1:18).

Elijah stepped into the fiery chariot and never died a normal death and Moses' when he died; his body was immediately buried by God and taken by an angel. I believe his body never saw the corruption of the grave. Now if this is the case, then their bodies will never ever see the corruption of the grave according to Revelation 11:12. And yet, they will be killed, resurrected, and taken up to heaven in a cloud just like the church will be caught up. And how Jesus departed in a cloud (Acts 1:9). Moses and Elijah are both under the Old Covenant. So they are not eligible for the New Covenant "catching up" of the church in the sense that a New Testament believer is. But God is going to resurrect and catch them up anyway (during the tribulation), because it is within his plan to do so. I believe Moses and Elijah may be exceptions to the rule (the corruption of the grave) because God knows he is going to bring them back during the tribulation period to die for his divine purpose. I also believe the fact that they are a type of the Word and the Spirit, God cannot allow the grave to have the victory over them because the Word and the Spirit are both eternal.

1 Corinthians 15:54-55 KJV
So when this corruptible shall have put on incorruption, and this mortal shall have

put on immortality, then shall be brought
to pass the saying that is written, Death
is swallowed up in victory. O death, where
is thy sting? O grave, where is thy victory?

Enoch walked with God and pleased him.

Genesis 5:24 KJV
And Enoch walked with God: and he was
not; for God took him.

The present day believer walks by faith and pleases
God. When Jesus comes back, believers will be changed,
translated, and caught up. It is by faith that we access all
the promises of God including the culmination or end of
our salvation which is the redemption of our bodies. Our
salvation and redemption begins when we are first saved
but the end of our salvation or the redemption of our
bodies happens at the return of the Lord for his church
(the rapture).

Romans 8:23 KJV
And not only they, but ourselves also,
which have the firstfruits of the Spirit,
even we ourselves groan within ourselves,
waiting for the adoption, to wit, the
redemption of our body.

Redemption is not exclusively a future event. It begins
when we first believe or when we are born again and
continues until we are resurrected. The seven Spirits

of God are sent forth into all the earth to facilitate our redemption and to make sure we have everything we need to get into eternity.

Enoch is a type of the New Covenant believer. He was a man of great faith. He is a type of the raptured believer.

> Hebrews 11:5-6, KJV
> By faith Enoch was translated that he should not see death; and was not found, because God had translated him: for before his translation he had this testimony, that he pleased God. But without faith it is impossible to please him: for he that cometh to God must believe that he is, and that he is a rewarder of them that diligently seek him.

Since Enoch is a type of the New Covenant believer he does not have to be brought back to eventually die. The New Covenant believer has the opportunity to live and never die.

> John 11:23-26 KJV
> Jesus saith unto her, Thy brother shall rise again. Martha saith unto him, I know that he shall rise again in the resurrection at the last day. Jesus said unto her, I am the resurrection, and the life: he that believeth in me, though he were dead, yet shall he live: And whosoever liveth and believeth in me shall never die. Believest thou this?

Jesus in this scripture is actually describing the resurrection at the rapture. Note that he says "though he were dead, yet shall he live", this is speaking of those who have died in Christ before he returns. These individuals are in the grave. "And whosoever live(s).....shall never die", is speaking of those who are and will be alive and in Christ when he comes (1 Thess. 4:13-18).

When God brings back Moses and Elijah as the two witnesses during the tribulation period, they will both die, be resurrected, and caught up to heaven before the entire world.

> Revelation 11:11-12 KJV
> And after three days and an half the Spirit of life from God entered into them, and they stood upon their feet; and great fear fell upon them which saw them. And they heard a great voice from heaven saying unto them, Come up hither. And they ascended up to heaven in a cloud; and their enemies beheld them.

The Two Olive Trees

Let's focus in on another area concerning Moses and Elijah and the two witnesses that I think is also very important. The book of Zechariah and the book of Revelation both mention the "two olive trees". Who or what are these two olive trees? What do they represent? In Zechariah chapter 4, Zechariah received a visitation from an angel.

Zechariah 4:1-3 KJV
And the angel that talked with me came again, and waked me, as a man that is wakened out of his sleep, And said unto me, What seest thou? And I said, I have looked, and behold a candlestick all of gold, with a bowl upon the top of it, and his seven lamps thereon, and seven pipes to the seven lamps, which are upon the top thereof: And two olive trees by it, one upon the right side of the bowl, and the other upon the left side thereof.

In the scriptures olive oil is a type of the Holy Spirit and the anointing of God. Olive trees represent the source of that oil or anointing.

Zechariah 4:11-14 KJV
Then answered I, and said unto him, What are these two olive trees upon the right side of the candlestick and upon the left side thereof? And I answered again, and said unto him, What be these two olive branches which through the two golden pipes empty the golden oil out of themselves? And he answered me and said, Knowest thou not what these be? And I said, No, my lord. Then said he, These are the two anointed ones, that stand by the Lord of the whole earth.

"The two anointed ones that stand by the Lord of the whole earth"? Sound familiar? Let's go back to the mount of transfiguration.

> Matthew 17:1-3 KJV
> And after six days Jesus taketh Peter, James, and John his brother, and bringeth them up into an high mountain apart, And was transfigured before them: and his face did shine as the sun, and his raiment was white as the light. And, behold, there appeared unto them Moses and Elias talking with him.

Moses and Elijah (Elias) are the two anointed ones standing by Jesus. This is a powerful reference to Jesus Christ and the power of the anointing of God. The two anointed ones represent the Word of God and the Spirit of God. Let's see what the final passage says about these two olive trees:

> Revelation 11:3-4 KJV
> And I will give power unto my two witnesses, and they shall prophesy a thousand two hundred and threescore days, clothed in sackcloth. These are the two olive trees, and the two candlesticks standing before the God of the earth.

We now know that the two witnesses are Moses and Elijah who represent or are a type of the Word and the Spirit. Remember, Jesus is the Word (John 1:1) but Moses is also a" type of Christ" in the scriptures. This qualifies him to be a type of the Word. This passage says the two witnesses are the two olive trees. The two olive trees are the source of the anointing in the earth. So we can safely say that the Word and the Spirit are the source of the anointing in the earth. God the Father is the ultimate source and the Word and the Spirit are eternally connected to the Father who is the source. And Jesus is the Word and he, the Father, and the Holy Ghost are one.

Again we see here that the scripture says that the two olive trees "stand by the God of all the earth". Who is the God of all the earth? Jesus, of course! Here we see a picture of the Word (Jesus) and the Holy Spirit standing by God the Father in the spiritual realm. In the natural we see Jesus (the God of all the earth) with Moses and Elijah standing by his side. As we can see here, there isn't only a dualistic power there is a shadow of heavenly things that we can see here.

> Revelation 4:5 KJV
> And out of the throne proceeded lightnings and thunderings and voices: and there were seven lamps of fire burning before the throne, which are the seven Spirits of God.

God the Father through the seven Spirits of God is the source of that anointing in heaven as we see them before the throne of God. The Holy Spirit through his sevenfold dimension bears witness in the earth.

1 John 5:6-9 KJV

This is he that came by water and blood,
even Jesus Christ; not by water only, but
by water and blood. And it is the Spirit
that beareth witness, because the Spirit is
truth. For there are three that bear record
in heaven, the Father, the Word, and the
Holy Ghost: and these three are one. And
there are three that bear witness in earth,
the Spirit, and the water, and the blood:
and these three agree in one. If we receive
the witness of men, the witness of God
is greater: for this is the witness of God
which he hath testified of his Son.

We can safely say that the Spirit of Truth is active in
bearing witness in the earth. Again we see here a shadow
effect between heaven and earth. But we also see that
"what" we see in heaven is not exactly what we see on
earth. So we see a shadow on earth. Shadows are not
always clear or well defined.

Let's move on to another point I'd like to touch on.

Matthew 5:16-18 KJV

Let your light so shine before men, that
they may see your good works, and glorify
your Father which is in heaven. Think not
that I am come to destroy the law, or the
prophets: I am not come to destroy, but to
fulfil. For verily I say unto you, Till heaven
and earth pass, one jot or one tittle shall

in no wise pass from the law, till all be
fulfilled.

It seems to me that many individuals in the body of
Christ have a problem with the law. And subsequently
have a problem with Moses. I believe that one of the roots
of the denial of Moses as one of the two witnesses is rooted
in this issue. This is because of the effects of the law on
our sinful nature. The apostle Paul expresses the details
of the struggle in his letters to the churches. But the Lord
has a different view of the law. As you can see, Jesus did
not come to do away with the law but to fulfil it.

> Psalms 19:7-10, KJV
> The law of the LORD is perfect,
> converting the soul: the testimony of the
> LORD is sure, making wise the simple.
> The statutes of the LORD are right,
> rejoicing the heart: the commandment of
> the LORD is pure, enlightening the eyes.
> The fear of the LORD is clean, enduring
> for ever: the judgments of the LORD are
> true and righteous altogether. More to be
> desired are they than gold, yea, than much
> fine gold: sweeter also than honey and the
> honeycomb.

After reading this passage there is nothing more to
say about whether the law is bad or good. The law is good;
man's sin nature is bad. Jesus came to fulfil the law so we
can receive the blessing of the God. We no longer have

to do the works of the law because we are people of faith in what Christ has done for us in fulfilling the law. If we have a problem with the law the devil knows that we will stumble at his Word in other areas.

I believe the enemy doesn't want you to see the fact that the Father, the Word, and the Holy Ghost are ready, willing, and able to supply you with every bit of power and anointing that you need to overcome the enemy in any situation. The enemy thinks if he can chip away or water down the written Word, then maybe one day he may be able cause someone to miss out on God's power. The Father, the Son, through the sevenfold dimension of the Holy Spirit along with all the angels of heaven at their command, are ready and waiting to hear our prayer and to show themselves strong in our midst, and on our behalf.

> John 14:10-11 KJV
> Believest thou not that I am in the Father, and the Father in me? the words that I speak unto you I speak not of myself: but the Father that dwelleth in me, he doeth the works. Believe me that I am in the Father, and the Father in me: or else believe me for the very works' sake.

The Holy Spirit bears witness of the Word of God in the earth. He confirms the Word with signs, wonders, miracles, and mighty deeds. The Holy Spirit is bearing witness of the truth. He is the Spirit of Truth. This is why we must always speak and minister the truth. This is one of the keys to the manifestation of the power of God. We must always minister the truth of God's Word otherwise the power of God may be thwarted from accomplishing what it ought to accomplish.

Finally if you have a problem with the law of God, Moses, or any type of authority, you need to get free so you can move forward in the power of God. There is a dualistic power that we have and that is the power of the Word and the Spirit of God.

The Seven Horns and Seven Eyes Sent into all the Earth

Revelation 5:6 KJV
And I beheld, and, lo, in the midst of the throne and of the four beasts, and in the midst of the elders, stood a Lamb as it had been slain, having seven horns and seven eyes, which are the seven Spirits of God sent forth into all the earth.

When were the seven Spirits of God sent forth into all the earth? The Holy Spirit is the full manifestation of the sevenfold Spirit of God. But when did each of them show up individually. There is still a pattern or order to when the seven Spirits of God were manifested in the earth. God held back on the full manifestation until a specific time. We need to take a look at each one to see when and where they show up in scripture.

1. The Spirit of Life appears in the beginning of creation (Genesis 1:2). And when Adam and Eve were created (Genesis 1:26, 2:7). The Spirit of Life

also shows up whenever someone is born again or wherever there is a resurrection or even miraculous healing, signs, and wonders.

2. The Spirit of Judgment manifest at the judgment of Adam and Eve and Cain. The Spirit of Judgment also manifests at the deliverance of the children of Israel from the bondage of Egypt and their exodus into the wilderness (Exodus 7:4). God judged Egypt with multiple plagues. He did this by the Spirit of Judgment. The Spirit of Judgment is also intricately involved in baptism (Isaiah 4:4).

3. The Spirit of Wisdom was here from the beginning (Proverbs 8:22). The Spirit of Wisdom was also given by God to the individuals who were assigned by him with the tasks of making the priests garments and building the tabernacle and all of its furnishings (Exodus 28:3, 31:3). I believe King Solomon also received the Spirit of Wisdom. We can receive the Spirit of Wisdom today if we ask without doubting (Eph. 1:17).

4. The Spirit of Prophecy is manifest all throughout the Old Testament. I believe the first time we see it is in the creation. God himself spoke the heavens, the earth, and the entire universe into existence. The first time the prophetic office is mentioned is in reference to Abraham (Genesis 20:7).

5. The Spirit of Glory first appeared to the children of Israel in Genesis 16:10. It also appeared on Mount Sinai to Moses (Exodus 24:16-18). It also filled Tabernacle and the Temple (Exodus 40:34, 1 Kings 8:11). God manifested his Glory at different

times. The aim of the building of the tabernacle and the temple were to allow him to manifest his glory as the children of Israel were obedient to him.

6. In the Old Testament the Spirit of Grace was not fully manifested as it is now. Specific individuals found grace in Gods sight, such as Noah (Genesis 6:8), Moses, and the children of Israel (Exodus 33:16). But the common man was still under the law, so the Spirit of Grace was not in its full manifestation until Jesus came (Hebrews 10:29). The Spirit of Grace facilitates this dispensation of Grace.

7. The Spirit of Truth was not fully revealed and manifested until Jesus left the earth after his resurrection. Jesus is the way, the truth, and the life (John 14:6). In John 14:17, 15:26, and 16:13 Jesus speaks of the Spirit of Truth. The Spirit of Truth could not come until Jesus (the Truth) was caught up to the Father.

So when did God send the seven Spirits of God into all the earth? We know that the Holy Spirit was here from the beginning. Actually he has no beginning. He is the full manifestation of the seven Spirits of God. If you study scripture closely, you will notice that the Holy Spirit manifest himself in multiple ways. But what I am referring to is when we saw the different manifestations of the Seven Spirits operating in the earth in the Bible.

Just to recap, we can see that the Spirit of God manifest himself in the Old Testament as 5 of the seven

Spirits. These five were out front in God's dealings with mankind:

- The Spirit of Life
- The Spirit of Judgment
- The Spirit of Wisdom
- The Spirit of Prophecy
- The Spirit of Glory

But notice, when we get to the New Testament, we see the Holy Spirit manifests in his full manifestation primarily as the following:

- The Sprit of Grace
- The Spirit of Truth

The following scriptures explain why we see this:

> John 1:14-17 (KJV)
> And the Word was made flesh, and dwelt among us, (and we beheld his glory, the glory as of the only begotten of the Father,) full of grace and truth. John bare witness of him, and cried, saying, This was he of whom I spake, He that cometh after me is preferred before me: for he was before me. And of his fulness have all we received, and grace for grace. For the law was given by Moses, but grace and truth came by Jesus Christ.

In the epistles to the churches the apostle Paul strongly emphasizes grace. But actually we are under both grace and truth. The seven Spirits of God were sent into the earth to bring us closer to God. The grace of God is the means by which God initially brings us to himself. The Spirit of Grace is the catalyst by which God accomplishes this in the earth. We are filled by the Spirit of Truth. He leads us into all truth. He causes us to walk in truth.

The Horns of Power

Revelation 1:4 KJV
John to the seven churches which are in Asia: Grace be unto you, and peace, from him which is, and which was, and which is to come; and from the seven Spirits which are before his throne;

Revelation 4:5KJV
And out of the throne proceeded lightnings and thunderings and voices: and there were seven lamps of fire burning before the throne, which are the seven Spirits of God.

Revelation 3:1KJV
And unto the angel of the church in Sardis write; These things saith he that hath the seven Spirits of God, and the seven stars; I know thy works, that thou hast a name that thou livest, and art dead.

Revelation 5:6 KJV
And I beheld, and, lo, in the midst of the
throne and of the four beasts, and in the
midst of the elders, stood a Lamb as it had
been slain, having seven horns and seven
eyes, which are the seven Spirits of God
sent forth into all the earth.

From the preceding scriptures we see a fivefold list of
attributes of the seven Spirits of God.

- They are before the throne of God
- They are also seven lamps of fire burning (they
  are light)
- Jesus has the seven Spirits of God
- They are the seven horns and seven eyes of the
  Lamb (Jesus)
- They are or were "sent forth" into all the earth
  (being "sent" means that they operate in an
  "apostolic" dimension).

The Holy Spirit through the seven Spirits of God is
currently in several places. He is in the Father, he is in
Jesus, who is in the Father and the Father in him, and he
is before the throne of God, and he was sent forth into
all the earth to fill all things including us. He appears
there before the throne as seven lamps burning before the
throne (Rev. 4:5). We also see seven lamps or candlesticks
mentioned in the book of Zechariah the prophet in the
Old Testament. The seven Spirits of God are the light of
the throne of God. God the Father is the source of that

light. That light proceeds from the Father. The scripture lets us know that Jesus is the light of the world. He also has the seven Spirits of God. They are the seven horns and seven eyes of the Lamb (Jesus).

The Lord Jesus was sent, the Holy Spirit was sent, the apostles were sent, and we are sent. The words "sent forth" in the following passage are translated from the same root word of the word "apostle". The seven Spirits are sent and operate in an apostolic dimension.

> Revelation 5:6 KJV
> And I beheld, and, lo, in the midst of the throne and of the four beasts, and in the midst of the elders, stood a Lamb as it had been slain, having seven horns and seven eyes, which are the seven Spirits of God sent forth into all the earth.

What do the "horns" represent in this passage? We must not overlook the horns' significance. In the Old Testament, in the Strong's definition of the word translated "horn" has a sevenfold meaning.

Here is the list:

1. A horn
2. A flask, cornet
3. Power
4. An elephants tooth
5. A peak of a mountain
6. A corner of the altar
7. A ray of light

As you can see, the word "horn" is included in that sevenfold definition. We are going to focus on two of the items in that list. The first one we have already mentioned and already explained in detail, which is the word "light". It's interesting that one of the meanings of the word "horn" is light. When I think of electricity I think of light and power. We showed earlier in this writing that light has a dualistic nature. So I'm not going to go into detail about it here. The second is the word "power". So the seven horns of the seven Spirits of God represent power and authority. Now we are going to discuss the dual aspects of power in the scriptures. In the New Testament the Greek word for "power" is also translated into the word "authority". There are two different Greek words that are actually used in that translation. The word "exousia" is translated most of the time into the words "authority" and "power". The Greek word "dunamis" is almost always translated into the words "power", "mighty works", "miracle", and sometimes "virtue" or "strength". The Greek word "dunamis" is where we get the word "dynamite" from. This revelation has been evident for quite a few years now, but truth never gets old.

A police officer has authority (exousia) with his badge and "dunamis" or dynamite power with his gun. We can clearly see a dualistic enforcement of power in this example. If an unlawful person does not respect the authority of the badge, he will have to deal with the dynamite power of the gun. This is the way it is today, God is giving mankind the opportunity to submit to the authority of his Word which is the Bible. But, there is coming a day when he will judge those who are rebelling against him. He will destroy them with his "dunamis" power.

In the following verse we can see how the Lord used his spiritual authority and dynamic power to deal with the unclean spirits that were oppressing the people.

> Luke 4:36 KJV
> And they were all amazed, and spake among themselves, saying, What a word is this! for with authority and power he commandeth the unclean spirits, and they come out.

So how does this line up with the horns of the seven Spirits of God? Again there is a dualistic point of reference in the revelation of the fact that Jesus has the seven Spirits of God. They are the seven horns and the seven eyes sent forth into all the earth. The horns represent his power, it is the ability he has to save and deliver us out of the "worst" of the worst situations.

> Luke 1:68-69 KJV
> Blessed be the Lord God of Israel; for he hath visited and redeemed his people,
> And hath raised up an horn of salvation for us in the house of his servant David;

Zacharias spoke this prophecy after he was filled with the spirit and his tongue was loosed. He was prophesying of Jesus in this prophecy and then about his son, John the Baptist. Jesus is the "horn of salvation" in this passage.

Psalms 18:2 KJV
The LORD is my rock, and my fortress,
and my deliverer; my God, my strength,
in whom I will trust; my buckler, and the
horn of my salvation, and my high tower.

A horn represents power, strength, and the ability to
be able to deliver and set free. The seven Spirits of God
are sent into the all the earth as the seven horns to deliver
us from everything that is in the earth that can harm us
and keep us in bondage.

Psalms 18:3, KJV
I will call upon the LORD, [who is worthy]
to be praised: so shall I be saved from mine
enemies.

Keep in mind that our heavenly Father is all power.
He is the ultimate power; as a matter of fact he is Power.

Matthew 26:64, KJV
Jesus saith unto him, Thou hast said:
nevertheless I say unto you, Hereafter
shall ye see the Son of man sitting on the
right hand of power, and coming in the
clouds of heaven.

The word translated power here is the Greek word
"dunamis". The right hand of power is the right hand of
God the Father.

Mark 16:19, KJV
So then after the Lord had spoken unto them, he was received up into heaven, and sat on the right hand of God.

The seven Spirits of God extend Gods power into all the earth. Since the Holy Spirit is omnipresent then God's power is omnipresent. Jesus is also power and he has the seven Spirits of God so he has all power.

Matthew 28:18, KJV
And Jesus came and spake unto them, saying, All power is given unto me in heaven and in earth.

Jesus is speaking of his authoritative power in this verse. Can you see the dualistic nature of power here? It's like the one two punch of the champion boxer, the left and right hand. The right hand normally is the strongest hand. Most left handed people end up using their right hand also. Some end up being able to use both hands equally. You've never seen a successful boxer that only punches with his right hand, or just one hand. But God does not have to always use all of his power.

Luke 11:20, KJV
But if I with the finger of God cast out devils, no doubt the kingdom of God is come upon you.

Jesus is speaking here in this passage.

So why do most Christians have so many problems accessing the power of God in their lives? I believe because many ministers do not know how to access the power and anointing of the Holy Spirit for miracles, healing, mighty signs, and wonders. And because of this many others in the body of Christ struggle. Some make excuses for why this person did not get healed or why this one died. Some even come up with theological reasons why the power of God is not working for them. Remember this, man and woman of God, it doesn't matter how good you preach or how nice you dress or how big your church is or how loud you scream at the devil. There are three major areas that must be addressed; holiness, humility, and faith. I'm not saying that we should one day have no fruit in this area and the next day we should see an abundance of miracles. This is a learning process and we need to begin to walk in this area and not worry about what others think or do. Are you a preacher or in ministry? Then you need to preach and teach the truth. We need to have a never ceasing desire to see God get the glory in every situation. And we need to make sure we are walking in the place God has for us and doing everything we know to do and the Lord will bless us.

The seven Spirits of God were sent and are here to help us destroy the works of the devil. The scripture clearly lets us know that we will see the power of God if we have faith and believe the Word of God.

Mark 16:17-18, KJV
And these signs shall follow them that believe; In my name shall they cast out

devils; they shall speak with new tongues;
They shall take up serpents; and if they
drink any deadly thing, it shall not hurt
them; they shall lay hands on the sick, and
they shall recover.

We must believe that the Lord has the power to deliver us from anything. Death is our greatest enemy. Jesus has already defeated death, but death has not been destroyed yet. The Lord is going to destroy death last after he has put every other enemy down.

> 1 Corinthians 15:21-26 KJV
> For since by man came death, by man came also the resurrection of the dead. For as in Adam all die, even so in Christ shall all be made alive. But every man in his own order: Christ the firstfruits; afterward they that are Christ's at his coming. Then cometh the end, when he shall have delivered up the kingdom to God, even the Father; when he shall have put down all rule and all authority and power. For he must reign, till he hath put all enemies under his feet. The last enemy that shall be destroyed is death.

Jesus combats ungodly demonic authority with his authority, and he confronts demonic power with his power. Death is what mankind fears the most. Since Jesus has already defeated death, it cannot harm the child of God the way that it destroys the sinner. When a born again child of God dies it is as if he has gone to sleep. When the sinner dies they are locked into eternal death, forever. There are no more opportunities to repent and follow after God once they pass on into eternity.

But, there is one way that is beyond their reach, there is another door if someone chooses to open it. Very few have chosen these days to open that door. There is an opportunity for a sinner to die and get a chance to live again. That way is manifested if that person is resurrected from the dead. I'm not talking about the rapture or the resurrection in the last day. I'm speaking of a "now" resurrection. The point when spiritual authority and power are manifested. Jesus demonstrated that power when he raised Lazarus from the dead. The horn of the Spirit of Life facilities any and every resurrection. But remember the seven Spirits of God are submissive to the Father and the Son. So whatever the Father says the Son does and whatever the Son says the Holy Spirit does. God is not the God of the dead, but he is the God of the living (Mark 12:27).

The Eyes of the Lord

Revelation 5:6 KJV
And I beheld, and, lo, in the midst of the throne and of the four beasts, and in the midst of the elders, stood a Lamb as it had been slain, having seven horns and seven eyes, which are the seven Spirits of God sent forth into all the earth.

2 Chronicles 16:9 KJV
For the eyes of the LORD run to and
fro throughout the whole earth, to shew
himself strong in the behalf of them whose
heart is perfect toward him…………

Zechariah 4:10 KJV
For who hath despised the day of small
things? for they shall rejoice, and shall see
the plummet in the hand of Zerubbabel
with those seven; they are the eyes of the
LORD, which run to and fro through the
whole earth.

The seven eyes of the Lord were first mentioned in
the book of Zechariah chapter three. Let's take a look at
that passage.

Zechariah 3:8-9, KJV
Hear now, O Joshua the high priest, thou,
and thy fellows that sit before thee: for they
are men wondered at: for, behold, I will
bring forth my servant the BRANCH. For
behold the stone that I have laid before
Joshua; upon one stone shall be seven
eyes: behold, I will engrave the graving
thereof, saith the LORD of hosts, and I
will remove the iniquity of that land in
one day.

The "BRANCH" in these verses is Jesus Christ. He is also the stone with the seven eyes that is laid before Joshua the high priest. The book of Daniel speaks of a stone also.

> Daniel 2:34-35, KJV
> Thou sawest till that a stone was cut out without hands, which smote the image upon his feet [that were] of iron and clay, and brake them to pieces. Then was the iron, the clay, the brass, the silver, and the gold, broken to pieces together, and became like the chaff of the summer threshingfloors; and the wind carried them away, that no place was found for them: and the stone that smote the image became a great mountain, and filled the whole earth.

Daniels prophecy is a prophecy of the end times and the stone is another prophetic reference to Jesus Christ at his second coming. Now when we read these passages in the book of Zechariah we begin to get more understanding of what is happening. The stone is Jesus and the seven eyes are the seven Spirits of God.

> Zechariah 4:1-3, KJV
> And the angel that talked with me came again, and waked me, as a man that is wakened out of his sleep, And said unto me, What seest thou? And I said, I have looked, and behold a candlestick all of

gold, with a bowl upon the top of it, and his seven lamps thereon, and seven pipes to the seven lamps, which are upon the top thereof: And two olive trees by it, one upon the right side of the bowl, and the other upon the left side thereof.

Now again, we see the seven lamp candlestick. We saw this in the book of revelation. Next to it are two olive trees. These two olive trees are the Word and the Spirit.

Zechariah 4:11-14, KJV

Then answered I, and said unto him, What are these two olive trees upon the right side of the candlestick and upon the left side thereof? And I answered again, and said unto him, What be these two olive branches which through the two golden pipes empty the golden oil out of themselves? And he answered me and said, Knowest thou not what these be? And I said, No, my lord. Then said he, These are the two anointed ones, that stand by the Lord of the whole earth.

As I stated in the previous chapter, the two olive trees represent these two anointed ones which are the two witnesses in the book of Revelation who are Moses and Elijah. But they represent the Word and the Spirit.

Revelation 11:4, KJV
These are the two olive trees, and the two
candlesticks standing before the God of
the earth.

Matthew 17:1-3, KJV
And after six days Jesus taketh Peter, James,
and John his brother, and bringeth them
up into an high mountain apart, And was
transfigured before them: and his face did
shine as the sun, and his raiment was white
as the light. And, behold, there appeared
unto them Moses and Elias talking with him.

Again Moses and Elijah represent the law and the
prophets which represent the Word and the Spirit. The
two olive trees represent the Word and the Spirit. The
olive oil represents the anointing of God. The Word and
the Spirit pour the anointing into the candlesticks which
are the eyes of the Lord. Notice that the Word and the
Spirit are connected to the same seven eyes. The scripture
says that Jesus has the seven Spirits of God and that the
seven Spirits of God are the eyes of the Lord.

Zechariah 4:5-7, KJV
Then the angel that talked with me
answered and said unto me, Knowest thou
not what these be? And I said, No, my
lord. Then he answered and spake unto
me, saying, This is the word of the LORD
unto Zerubbabel, saying, Not by might,

nor by power, but by my spirit, saith the
LORD of hosts. Who art thou, O great
mountain? before Zerubbabel thou shalt
become a plain: and he shall bring forth
the headstone thereof with shoutings,
crying, Grace, grace unto it.

This is probably one of my favorite passages. God is
saying here that nothing has power like the power of his
Holy Spirit. The Holy Spirit manifests that power by the
seven Spirits of God. I believe this is the main reason the
Lord has given me this revelation and the main reason for
the writing of this book. God wants his power displayed in
these last days. Remember that I said that Enoch is a type of
the New Testament Christian. The Lord has showed me that
this is the generation of an Enoch type of believer. Enoch
walked with God in such a manner that God took him.

Hebrews 11:5, KJV
By faith Enoch was translated that he
should not see death; and was not found,
because God had translated him: for before
his translation he had this testimony, that
he pleased God.

Enoch was raptured just as the New Testament believer
will be raptured. But how does a person please God?

Hebrews 11:6, KJV
But without faith it is impossible to please
him: for he that cometh to God must

believe that he is, and that he is a rewarder
of them that diligently seek him.

Notice, these two verses are actually connected, one
after another. This confirms my point that we are in
the era of an Enoch type of faith and God wants us to
understand that we have all the power that we need to
accomplish the work that he has called us to.

2 Chronicles 16:9 KJV
For the eyes of the LORD run to and
fro throughout the whole earth, to shew
himself strong in the behalf of them
whose heart is perfect toward him.........

A perfect heart is a heart that believes God. The seven
Spirits of God are running to and fro throughout the whole
earth searching for someone who has faith so that the Lord
can show himself strong towards them. The eyes of the Lord
see our dilemma, but faith moves the hand of God to deliver.

Zechariah 4:10, KJV
For who hath despised the day of small
things? for they shall rejoice, and shall see
the plummet in the hand of Zerubbabel
with those seven; they are the eyes of the
LORD, which run to and fro through the
whole earth.

Faith is what connects us to the power of God. The
seven Spirits of God are looking for faith throughout the

whole earth. Some Christians don't believe this. They don't think we need faith. Jesus said on multiple occasions "by your faith you have been made whole". Faith pleases God and moves the hand of God. Fasting doesn't move God as much as it builds our faith when we deny our flesh. Some feel that the more or longer you fast the more faith you automatically have. This is not true. People in the world fast and some fast longer and more often than most Christians. But they have no faith. Why? Because there are principles of faith that must be followed in order to walk in faith. Faith must be carried out, walked out, or executed.

The Seven Spirits of God: The Execution of His Power

The Execution

Matthew 17:14-21, KJV

And when they were come to the multitude, there came to him a certain man, kneeling down to him, and saying, Lord, have mercy on my son: for he is lunatick, and sore vexed: for ofttimes he falleth into the fire, and oft into the water. And I brought him to thy disciples, and they could not cure him. Then Jesus answered and said, O faithless and perverse generation, how long shall I be with you? how long shall I suffer you? bring him hither to me. And Jesus rebuked the devil; and he departed out of him: and the child was cured from that very hour. Then came the disciples to Jesus apart, and said, Why could not we cast him out? And Jesus said unto them, Because of your unbelief: for verily I say unto you, If ye have faith as a grain of mustard seed, ye shall say unto this mountain, Remove hence to yonder place; and it shall remove; and nothing shall be impossible unto you. Howbeit this kind goeth not out but by prayer and fasting.

Obviously you can see after reading this passage that there was a problem with execution among the disciples. It had gotten to the point that the Lord was frustrated with them and their lack of faith. I don't think that the problem got much better because the disciples still hadn't prioritized prayer over sleep at the Garden of Gethsemane. But we saw a distinct change after the Lord's resurrection and after they were filled with the Holy Ghost.

In order to have the power of God manifested in your life and ministry, you must execute the things in your life that build your faith.

Hebrews 11:1, KJV
Now faith is the substance of things hoped for, the evidence of things not seen.

I believe the Holy Spirit gave me this interpretation of this passage. "Faith becomes the thing you hope for until you get it".

Romans 4:17, KJV
(As it is written, I have made thee a father of many nations,) before him whom he

believed, even God, who quickeneth the
dead, and calleth those things which be
not as though they were.

God spoke the world into existence. The pattern of
faith is to follow the Lord's example and "call those things
that be not as though they were". We must believe the Word
of God. Then we must speak the Word with corresponding
action. We must first deal with our unbelief. The best way
to do that is by prayer and fasting. Fasting alone does not
move God. Faith in God moves God. Fasting helps you
to believe the Lord, builds your faith, and deals with your
flesh. When you fast you put your flesh under submission.

Faith does not look at the circumstances or the
symptoms, but it looks at the Word of God. So there
is a process to getting strong faith. The seven Spirits of
God were sent into the world to make sure you are well
equipped to destroy the works of the devil. But you must
execute.

The disciples were following Jesus. They were with
him every day. They slept with him, they ate with him.
They went where he went. They saw all the things he did.
He demonstrated to them the process. But for some reason
at that time it didn't totally click. The Lord Jesus held up
a standard. He let them see his frustration with their lack
of faith but he didn't have a nasty attitude about it. They
had a desire to move in the power of God, so they came
to him and asked him to tell them what the problem was.
He calmly told them. It's "your unbelief". We need the
same desire to see the power of God move in our lives. I
do believe they had enough faith to cast out some demons

though. That's why they kept trying. Also, earlier on when he called the twelve he gave them power (authority) to do that very thing.

> Matthew 10:1, KJV
> And when he had called unto him his twelve disciples, he gave them power against unclean spirits, to cast them out, and to heal all manner of sickness and all manner of disease.

So they were casting out demons and healing the sick but this particular one was a tough one. This is why Jesus said "this kind goeth not out but by prayer and fasting".

Many see Jesus in their minds though a filtered mindset. Many look at scripture and water them down into something that is powerless. But it still might sound good, but there is no power. I was watching a popular preacher on TV and he began to explain a scripture that I am very familiar with and he deliberately changed the whole context to make a point. This disturbed me. His final point was true but the way he got there was not. We have to be very careful with this when teaching God's Word. Our faith is based on the truth not a scripture that we have misconstrued twisted to fit our discussion. We have the Spirit of Truth to keep us walking in the truth. We must preach and teach the truth of the Word of God. We should never water down the Word to make a point. To start with, you must believe and stick with the truth of the Word. You must study and believe the entire Word of God. John in the book of Revelation swallowed the whole book (Rev. 10:9).

Prayer is the next thing that needs execution. The Spirit of Grace is here to help us with our prayer lives. I've gotten into a lot of trouble in my walk with the Lord because of a lack of prayer. If you do not consistently pray you will stumble and maybe even fall in this Christian walk. You will end up in the flesh and wonder how you got there. I believe this is one of the areas the devil fights us the most, our prayer lives. It is the point of inception. He fights us at that key point. He fights us at the foundation. He knows that if he can keep you from praying, half the battle is won.

Whenever I am obedient to the Word and spend time in a season of prayer, miracles signs and wonders always follow. Do I need to repeat that? Let me say it this way, when you spend time in prayer and fasting you are being prepared for God to use you mightily. The opportunities to pray for others begin to increase and it is so awesome to be "prayed up" and prepared for the challenge.

Let me speak to many new ministers, preachers, teachers, evangelists, pastors, prophets, and even apostles. One of the first things that you will encounter is the desire to see people fall down under the power of God when you pray for them. Nobody wants to write or talk about these things but I believe the Holy Spirit is leading me to write about this subject. I know, because I've been there and I understand the desire to be used by God. Falling down accomplishes nothing if the persons spiritual needs are not met. When I was a new minister I struggled with this. I would pray for people and nothing happened or they would cry or I was so focused on them falling down that don't think I ministered to their needs. And the Holy Spirit was not pleased. Some even get to the point where they even push people down. I didn't do that, but I was tempted to. If you push people down, you are looking for all the glory. Some people that you pray for will also fall down by their own power without the anointing (they do this for several reasons that I'm not going to discuss at this time). You see, we are here to work together with the Holy Ghost. We are not here to do what we want and disregard his leading. So after a while of doing things my way without any results I submitted to the will of God and I told the Lord these words, "Lord, I don't care if a person falls down or not. If they fall good, if they don't that's ok too. I just want you to get the glory". Well, that was when the power of God began to move in my ministry. I submitted to the will of God. I submitted to the seven Spirits of God and began to see the manifestations (even though I had not received the full revelation I have now of the seven Spirits of God).

My Testimonies

The first incident surprised me. I was praying for my older brother in the living room of my apartment when he fell back on the couch stiff as a board. He looked like he was still standing but he was lying on the couch. To be honest I thought he was faking. But I realized that no one could lie in the position he was in for that long and stay stiff the way he did. Sometimes God will do something right in front of our eyes and we still stumble at what we see. He then he woke up he had no idea he was out under the power of God. To God be the glory.

The next time the power of God was manifested is

when I was called to preach at a church where I knew the pastor. But the pastor was away. So, I taught a word to the congregation and gave an altar call for prayer. Only one young man came up. I asked him what he needed prayer for. He said he wanted prayer for his family and his wife and he wanted to be the man of God that God wanted him to be. I said ok and I began to pray for him. I then laid hands on him and he began to fall backward. I didn't realize he was falling until it was too late for me to catch him. My eyes were closed but when I opened them, I said out loud "oh, oh!" But, nobody was behind him. As I watched and the congregation watched, this man fell backward in slow motion. He fell very slowly like someone was holding him and gently laid him on the floor. Again, he was also stiff as a board like he was still standing. It seemed like he fell into a bed of feathers. When he got close to the floor, he touched down very softly. I was stunned along with the congregation. I looked at them and they looked at me, and we all had our mouths open in amazement. Then another man came up and I didn't expect him to fall but God had me to prophecy to him and lay hands on him and he was truly blessed.

After that I went to a conference in Delaware. It was a Sunday school and youth convention. I felt in my spirit that God was going to use me to minister. But I wasn't one of the speakers. So I said "well Lord your will be done". Just before the service the Overseer came to me and said "I want you to pray for people after the preaching". So when the sermon was over all the ministers got up to pray and minister to the congregation. Well, all the glory goes to God. Every single person that I laid hands on fell under the power of God so much that the other ministers stopped praying and came over to catch those that I was ministering to. This was a great show of humility on their part. I'm sure the Lord blessed them for that. Humility is one of the keys to allowing the power of God to move in our midst.

After that the Lord began to deal with me on specifics on how to really cast out demons and get people healed. He showed me different details about the things that Jesus did and said.

Then I began to see things happen while I ministered to people. For example, I wore glasses at the time. Now I wear contacts. Sometimes I don't think I need them. My eyes have gotten better over the years instead of worse. Anyway, when I would minister at the altar, my glasses would become drenched with oil. At first I thought it was me. Because I had a tendency to have oily skin, but I realized after a while that it was not me but it was the anointing of the Holy Spirit. It looked just like olive oil. My fellow ministers on the altar were constantly cleaning my glasses to try and get the oil off of them while I was ministering. God is amazing.

Then another specific incident happened when I would get around people especially the unsaved. When I would go to the bank, on a regular basis, whenever I went to the counter the bank tellers would start weeping uncontrollably. Tears would continually flow from their eyes. They would struggle to take my deposit. I would minister to them the best I could but there was always someone waiting in line behind me. These are a few of the manifestations I experienced when I began to yield to the Holy Spirit.

I had one incident with a member of my church. After

service I would always chat and minister to individuals in the congregation. One day I was chatting with a young woman and when I turned to look at her she jumped back. It surprised me that she did that. I thought something was wrong because her eyes got wide and she literally reacted. A little while later she called me and she said, "Pastor, do you remember that day we were talking and I reacted to you "I said "Yes." She said, "When you looked at me, beams of light shot out of your eyes at me". I was in awe. I didn't have a clue why she reacted like that that day but now I knew. Praise God.

At other times while I was ministering at the altar, I wouldn't even have to touch people. The anointing and the power of God was so intense and thick that the people were falling before I touched them. I mean literally I would get my hand 3-4 inches from them and they would fall. One of the ministers in my church said to me "Pastor, you're not even touching them". It's funny; I didn't even realize it until she said something. The power of God is tangible. It has force. It can knock you down and lift you up. I remember one time I was in a service with a friend of mine who was a prophet and we started praying at the end of the service. The power God came out of nowhere and began to lift me up off the ground. The prophet began to say "Jesus, Jesus, glory, glory". Meanwhile he was holding my hand and holding me down. I was literally on my toes with my back arched and I felt like I was going to flip over the podium which was behind us on a platform.

I heard a preacher say "when the power of God comes in contact with us something has to give and it won't be the power of God".

I will reiterate again that whenever I spend time in a season of prayer miracles signs and wonders always, always, always follow. I prayed for a young lady who had HIV/AIDS. I was told her T cell count was dropping fast. I met with her at the church and the whole time in that meeting all I did was cry. The compassion of the Lord enveloped and saturated me. Jesus showed this type of compassion when he healed individuals when he was here. I prayed for her and then she actually moved away and we didn't hear from her anymore. Then a while later I found out that she had a baby and the baby did not have HIV/AIDS, neither did the baby's father or neither did she test positive for HIV anymore. Praise God. It was such a blessing to hear this.

There was another young lady that was pregnant and she found out that her baby had Down syndrome. They found it through certain tests. This young lady's father was a bishop and she felt like she was under condemnation because he said that she bought shame to his ministry. The baby was conceived out of wedlock. Well, God is a forgiving and compassionate God and he doesn't care what people think, even his leaders sometimes. Healing someone is just as easy as forgiving someone to God.

> Matthew 9:2-5, KJV
> And, behold, they brought to him a man sick of the palsy, lying on a bed: and Jesus seeing their faith said unto the sick of the palsy; Son, be of good cheer; thy sins be forgiven thee. And, behold, certain of the scribes said within themselves, This man blasphemeth. And Jesus knowing their

thoughts said, Wherefore think ye evil in
your hearts? For whether is easier, to say,
Thy sins be forgiven thee; or to say, Arise,
and walk?

So the young lady came to church, (she was friends
with one of the ministers in the church). That Sunday
morning I can't remember if the Lord spoke to me or
he just impressed it on my heart to pray for her in the
beginning of the service. This was before we went into our
normal service. We had just started to sing and praise God.
This is why it is important to be led by the Holy Spirit.
Sometimes we want to stick to our order of service and not
let the Holy Spirit have his way. I called her up to the front
of the church as she was continually weeping the whole
time she was there. And when she got to the altar, in the
Spirit I saw the heavens open and the power God came
down from heaven and swirled around both of us as I laid
hands on her. It was so strong, sweet, beautiful, and pure.
To this day I have not had a similar experience (hopefully
I will in the future). She went back to the doctor and they
checked and found that the baby was healed and perfectly
healthy. They could not find any trace of Down syndrome.
She had the baby a few months later and he was the cutest
little guy I had ever seen, and had no signs of the disease.
Praise God.

One particular time the whole church was sick with
the flu. I wasn't sick. I didn't get everything that came
down the pike. So I was fine. I guess the anointing kept
me well. I got up from my chair and looked at everyone
in the congregation and they were miserable but they still

came to church. So I got the anointing oil and anointed every single sick person that was present and every one was healed. Praise God.

In that season the Lord led me to go to a women's conference in Baltimore, Maryland. I said to the Lord "why do I need to go to a women's conference?" But I knew he wanted me there. Well I soon found out why. While the well-known preacher was preaching, the anointing was so strong. There were more than five thousand women in that place. There were some men but mostly women. The women began to wail. I had never been in an atmosphere like that. Meanwhile all of a sudden I had an open vision. In other words, my eyes were open; I was not sleep or passed out under the anointing. The preacher and everything on the platform disappeared. I then saw myself on the platform. A little distance from me was a line forming with lame and crippled people with all kinds of ailments. All did was pray and point my hands at them and they were instantly healed and transformed before our eyes. Then, the scene shifted to a car accident where a person was fatally wounded. I went and laid hands on them and they opened their eyes. (This part is more graphic than this but I choose not to get into the details here). Now I knew why he sent me to that conference. He wanted to show me the things I thought were impossible and he wanted me to remember it.

One day my nephew called me and said he was traveling through and wanted to see me. So I went to meet with him and found out that he had a broken leg. He said it was a bad break. He slipped on some ice or something like that. Well, I prayed for him and didn't think about it much after that. I later received a call from his wife telling me that he went to the doctor and they said his bone has healed extremely fast and if I remember right they took of his cast. This is a true blessing. I also had a young man in my church that broke his arm. He was our drummer. I think he broke it playing basketball. I was closing service and he jumped up and said "Pastor, can you pray for me?" I said "of course" so I prayed for him. This was Sunday. Wednesday he came to church and his cast was off and he was completely healed. Broken bones seem to be healed easily by the anointing that God has given.

My son was messing around on the upstairs banister in our home. He climbed over the banister and was hanging upside down and lowering himself. He lost his grip and fell head first onto the first step of the stairs. It was a ten to twelve foot drop, maybe more or less. When I saw him lying at the bottom of the stairs, he had blood coming out of his mouth, nose, and ears. When his mother saw him she began to scream uncontrollably. I had to calm her down and then I went to pray for him. I took authority in the name of Jesus and spoke healing to his body. His eyes were swirling around in circles. When I prayed his eyes straightened instantly. Then I said to him "you're going to be alright" and he looked at me and shook his head yes. 911 had already been called. When they arrived they kept asking where did he fall from and I told them "up there at the top of the banister head first". They decided to LifeStar (helicopter) him to the hospital. Unfortunately, I had to take the trip with him. I'm not going talk about the helicopter ride right now. Whew, it was interesting. When he got there they immediately began brain scans, and all kinds of tests to check him out and he came through perfect with no problems. He was perfectly normal. He came home with us and didn't have to stay in the hospital. We gave our testimony in church the next service. Praise God. This particular miracle God did in spite of what I was feeling and dealing with at the time. But he is faithful.

I've seen the Spirit of Glory manifest in meetings also. I remember before I started pastoral ministry, the church I was a member of had a church convocation. I think I was one of moderators of the main service. I truly don't remember. What I do remember was all the ministers and our Overseer were on the podium when the glory of the Lord entered the house. The Spirit of Glory was so potent that everyone there was laid out. All I remember was I was on the floor and I could not get up until the Spirit of Glory lifted. At this time I knew nothing about the seven Spirits of God. But now I know what God's intention was. If we would have continued to yield to the Lord we would have experienced a mighty move of God.

> 1 Kings 8:10-11, KJV
> And it came to pass, when the priests were come out of the holy place, that the cloud filled the house of the LORD, So that the priests could not stand to minister because of the cloud: for the glory of the LORD had filled the house of the LORD.

Another point I'd like to piggy back on this scripture with is this; when I was first saved I would go up for prayer and I developed this desire to be prayed for and to fall under the power of God. But to my surprise it would not happen. I felt like something was wrong with me. Time after time there was nothing. Different ministers prayed for me, no results. I felt Gods power but nothing occurred. I asked the Lord what was going on but he never answered. Sometimes the Lord remains silent until we get to the place spiritually where we can understand. Then one day he showed me that he designed me in such a way that I would be able to stand under a very heavy anointing. The power of God in my life and ministry would be exceedingly great. Great grace is what I believe he was referring to when he showed me this (Acts 4:33). Afterwards I understood. There were times where I was one of the only ones standing when the power God fell.

Then there was a time in my life that was very tough. I am going to touch on this briefly but I'm not going to spend too much time on this. I went through a divorce. Then the enemy began to bring condemnation to my mind and he said I was washed up. God was upset with me and my ministry would never be anything and so on. At first I began to believe all that garbage but the Spirit of Truth had something else in mind, restoration. You see, he is our comforter. He walks with us and talks to us. He began to speak and I began to listen. We just have to decide who we are going to listen too. I decided to listen to the Spirit of Truth.

John 14:16-18, KJV
And I will pray the Father, and he shall give you another Comforter, that he may abide with you for ever; Even the Spirit

of truth; whom the world cannot receive,
because it seeth him not, neither knoweth
him: but ye know him; for he dwelleth
with you, and shall be in you. I will not
leave you comfortless: I will come to you.

If you are a child of God, you are never alone. The Spirit of Truth is there to show you the truth about who you are, what the Lord thinks about you and your situation, and what the Lord wants you to do. When we truly repent, the Holy Spirit does not brow beat us. He is focused on establishing the truth in our lives in order to bring us back to our purpose. Once again, after a season of fasting and prayer, the miracles began to happen again.

This is when the Lord began to speak to me about writing this book. Then I was at a church service and a well-known preacher kept staring at me while she preached. Then in the middle of her sermon she stops and looks at me and says "you need to write that book". And then she picks back up and finishes her message without missing a beat. I was stunned. The Lord was emphatic about the writing of this book. So I began to be obedient and here we are.

Then the miracles started again. I was coming home from work when I received a call from a bishop's wife who lived in North Carolina. She said her daughter was in the hospital and she needed prayer. I was very tired and I purposed in my mind to go to the hospital the next day. But the Holy Spirit said "no, go tonight". I was tired but I decided to be obedient to the Lord. I went in and took a shower and quickly got in my car and drove to the hospital.

On the way the Lord began to speak to me. He said he was going to heal her but he wanted me minister to her first. So when I got to her room, I told her who I was and I told her that God was going to heal her but we had to deal with her heart. She began to confess that she grew up in the church. When she was a young teen, a prophet came to her church and in front of the congregation said she was pregnant. This was not true. She was not pregnant. This person was a lying prophet. But here is the worst part, when she did not begin to show her pregnancy the church was sure she had an abortion and began to treat her terribly. On top of all that she was called to a prophetic ministry, but she had developed a hatred for church people. We needed to deal with the bitterness in her heart. Just as we were getting to that point, the nurse came in and asked me to step out into the waiting area. I did and the doctor went in and closed the door. About 15-20 minutes later the doctor left and they said I could go back in. When I walked back in she was facing the opposite wall with her back to me crying. I asked her what the doctor said. He told her in addition to the Stevens- Johnsons syndrome that she was diagnosed with; she had tumors in the blood vessels of her brain. Stevens- Johnsons syndrome is a rare disease where it looks like a person's skin is burning from the inside out. The mucous membranes get infected or it may be an adverse reaction to medication. It can be fatal. I found out later that this was the same disease Manute Bol, the former NBA star died from. When we worked through her forgiveness issue the Lord released me to pray for her. She was lying on the bed and I laid hands on her and prayed. While I was praying, the power of God hit her and she instantly rose up off the bed with her back arched and her arms spread like she was on a cross. She was overwhelmed with the power of God. I think her feet and legs were touching the bed but I couldn't tell because they were under the cover. I stepped back and let God do his work. After about 4 or 5 minutes she laid back down. And I blessed her and left. The next day I received a report that her skin was almost totally healed (it was pealing and looked infected) and the tumors in her brain were gone. Praise God, praise God, and praise God.

> Luke 4:36, KJV
> And they were all amazed, and spake among themselves, saying, What a word is this! for with authority and power he commandeth the unclean spirits, and they come out.

Now, let's begin to talk about demonic manifestations and the casting out of unclean spirits. Now I'm not going to spend too much time here because I've cast out plenty of demons but I don't like talking about it as much as I like talking about healing and miracles. One of the first manifestations I experienced was dramatic. When I first started pastoral ministry the church I was attending started a bible study in a town about 50 miles from where I lived. We were chosen by the leadership to plant a church in this location. This was the will of God. The devil was upset about this, so people got upset. But the bottom line is that God told the leadership to do it and they obeyed God. The woman that we were visiting was from Africa.

When we would come for bible study, it was very hard for me to teach or pray or do anything pertaining to the things of God in that house for some reason. At the end of one bible study the woman said "there is evil in my house, can you pray?" She was a single mother with a preteen daughter. They were both scared of the demonic activity that was occurring in their home. So I said "ok, we will pray". I had an older West Indian mother that was with me and she followed me through the house praying in the Spirit. As I went up the stairs I sensed in the Spirit that a demonic spirit flew out of an upstairs bedroom window. I knew we were dealing with a serious situation. When we went downstairs the woman of the house asked me to pray for her. One of the sisters that were with me had opened the front door that led to the outside. As soon as I began to pray the front door slammed and shut extremely hard, all the lights went out, and all the blinds opened up. Amazingly, I was not afraid of this entire scene. God had given me a calm peace and boldness. I just continued to pray in Jesus name. Others that were with me were afraid though. So we looked over in the corner of the living room and I notice a table covered with a cloth. I said to the sister "what is that?" I don't remember her response but it was basically a shrine. When we pulled the cover, she had a statue of the Virgin Mary, Buddha, Jesus, African statues, the Koran, the book of Mormon and all kinds of religious stuff. We told her that she had to get rid of that shrine and she did. The next time we came for bible study. There was a totally different atmosphere in that place. It was bright, sunny, and free. I was able to freely teach and pray. Praise God for his power and his deliverance.

Before this incident I had several incidents happen in my childhood. I'm not going to get into detail about those things but they produced two things in me; fear and this conclusion. I said in my heart "if there is this much evil, there must be good". So I had to confront my fear and here is the way the Lord had me to do it. I was engaged to be married. So I used to work in a very hot environment. When I got off work I would go home and shower and go see my fiancé. If I stayed too late I would get really tired because of the heat at my work place. I would get to the point that I was so sleepy I couldn't drive. So she asked her father could I stay there he said yes this time. In the past he always said no. They had a finished basement. So I slept on the couch down there. My fiancé had a little nephew that I just loved. He was quiet but playful sometimes. So I was lying on the couch and going to sleep when I felt someone playing with my ears, and my nose and gently tickling my face. I awoke but I did not open my eyes. I thought to myself this is her nephew messing with me. So I decided that I was going to scare him. I jumped up, opened my eyes and said "boo". To my surprise standing in front me was a demon in the form of a dog. It was standing on its hind legs in other words standing upright like a human. It had a snout and ears like a dog (German shepherd or Collie). It had eyes like a man and very sharp white teeth. It was also very black. It was about 3 to 4 feet tall. When it saw me it gasped and in turn I gasped. It turned and ran towards the basement wall. Just before it got to the wall it disappeared. Then an intense spirit of fear came upon me. I had never felt fear like this before. I struggled with it for a long time until I started to pray. Then deep down in my spirit I began to speak in tongues and that fear left. I then slept better than I had ever slept before. I've never felt that fear ever again.

I've had different manifestation where I was visited by demonic spirits. I was coming out of the church I pastored and our church was on the second floor. It had a long flight of stairs. I called it "the upper room". We had an agreement with the other tenants in the building that the last person to leave had to turn off the lights which were in a hallway closet. I turned off the lights in the church and locked the door. And then I went into the closet and turned off the lights and when I turned to walk out standing in front of me was a figure. He was about just under my height. He was opaque, so I saw him but I couldn't make out his facial features. I stood there for a moment and stared at him as he stared at me. But, once again, I had no fear. But then I surprised myself by the next thing I did. Instead of rebuking him, I laughed at him and walked down the stairs to my car. Sometimes the devil wants to scare you and get you all worked up in fear. God taught me something that day.

I had a time when I was going through a few things in my life and ministry. I had to make some hard decisions which bought on much hardship. But I know I was being led by the Spirit of the Lord. We had a young man in our church that could sing so well but he had problems with staying focused on the things of God and staying holy. He came to church one day and while we were having service he wouldn't come into the sanctuary. He stayed in the hallway. I think one of the members came and told me there was something wrong with him. I went out into the hallway and as soon as he saw me he says "you're not acting right". I said "excuse me". He said "I don't like the way you are acting". I looked him and asked him a question just by his answer I knew he had a demon. It's funny when you are making hard decisions and you are questioning whether you are doing the right thing. Then the devil speaks through a person and confirms that you are on the right track. The devil didn't like what I was doing because I was kicking him out. So I told the young man to go in the sanctuary and he obeyed. The demon obeyed everything I told him to do. I then told him to go to the front of the church and he did. I decided to use this as a teaching moment for those who never saw a demon cast out. The Lord led me to do it this way. When he got to the front of the sanctuary, the unclean spirit began to manifest. They often act up before they are going to get cast out. The young man got on one hand and balanced his entire body perfectly while arched his back and his legs on that hand. Now, this young man was not that athletic so we knew it was the demon giving him the ability to do it. After that I told the spirit to come out of him in the name of Jesus and it did.

These are a few examples of incidents I've had with dealing with demons and their strongholds. I've had to cast out demons on a regular basis over the years. It's almost a blur sometimes. But my whole purpose here in this final chapter is to help you to see God's ideal purpose when it comes to healing, miracles, and deliverance from the forces of darkness. I'm not trying to get the glory. I give all the glory to God. Without him I am nothing.

More Faith Teaching

So now I am going to give an overview of some key concepts. I may throw a few new things in to stir up your thinking. Jesus has delegated power (authority) to us. He has given us authority over the "dunamis" or dynamic power of the enemy. There is no power that is more powerful than the power of the Holy Spirit or specifically the seven Spirits of God.

> Luke 10:17-19, KJV
> And the seventy returned again with joy, saying, Lord, even the devils are subject unto us through thy name. And he said unto them, I beheld Satan as lightning fall from heaven. Behold, I give unto you power to tread on serpents and scorpions, and over all the power of the enemy: and nothing shall by any means hurt you.

Faith gives us access to that power. The eyes of the Lord which are the seven Spirits of God are searching throughout the earth looking for those who have faith. If we want to access the power of God we must build our faith.

> Mark 16:17-18, KJV
> And these signs shall follow them that believe; In my name shall they cast out devils; they shall speak with new tongues; They shall take up serpents; and if they

drink any deadly thing, it shall not hurt them; they shall lay hands on the sick, and they shall recover.

There is power in the name of Jesus. The Lord's name is powerful. His name is the name above all names. Sickness, disease, and demons know his name. And they bow to his name, when we have faith in the name of Jesus and believe nothing is impossible.

Every child of God has been given a measure of faith. What you do to build your faith is up to you. I spoke about prayer and how it builds your faith but we need to pray in tongues to build our faith. The disciples/apostles were transformed after the Lord's resurrection and after they were filled with the Holy Spirit.

> Acts 2:1-4, KJV
> And when the day of Pentecost was fully come, they were all with one accord in one place. And suddenly there came a sound from heaven as of a rushing mighty wind, and it filled all the house where they were sitting. And there appeared unto them cloven tongues like as of fire, and it sat upon each of them. And they were all filled with the Holy Ghost, and began to speak with other tongues, as the Spirit gave them utterance.

If you want to walk in the power of God, it is imperative that you are filled with the Holy Spirit. When you pray in tongues, you are charging your spirit man like one would charge a rechargeable battery.

Now the scripture says that Jesus has the seven Spirits of God. We do not have the seven Spirits of God like Jesus does. He possesses the seven Spirits without measure.

> John 3:34, KJV
> For he whom God hath sent speaketh the words of God: for God giveth not the Spirit by measure [unto him].

When we are filled with the Spirit, we are given the Spirit of Truth. Jesus is the only one in the scriptures that has the seven Spirits of God (Rev. 3:1, 5:6).

> Colossians 2:9, KJV
> For in him dwelleth all the fulness of the Godhead bodily.

Now, I'm sure that there are individuals that will disagree with me on this point. So, I'm going to break it down for you. When Jesus was here he did not operate in the full dimension of his glory. He operated as a man anointed by the Holy Ghost. How do we know this? Simply because, Jesus was and had to be anointed by God in order to do the work.

> Acts 10:38, KJV
> How God anointed Jesus of Nazareth with the Holy Ghost and with power: who went about doing good, and healing all that

were oppressed of the devil; for God was with him.

If he was operating in his full dimension of power and glory, he would not have needed to be anointed. We also know that he was not operating in his full dimension because he stripped himself before coming to earth to be born of a virgin.

> Philippians 2:6-8, KJV
> Who, being in the form of God, thought it not robbery to be equal with God: But made himself of no reputation, and took upon him the form of a servant, and was made in the likeness of men: And being found in fashion as a man, he humbled himself, and became obedient unto death, even the death of the cross.

So, we can see that the Lord did not operate in his full glory when he was here on earth. He operated as a man anointed by God because he was in the likeness and fashion of a man.

> Hebrews 10:5, KJV
> Wherefore when he cometh into the world, he saith, Sacrifice and offering thou wouldest not, but a body hast thou prepared me:

Jesus had a physical fleshly body just like ours except that he was without sin. We know also that he was not operating under his full glory and power because the scripture mentions only once when he let the glory shine. And that was at the Mount of Transfiguration.

> Matthew 17:1-2, KJV
> And after six days Jesus taketh Peter, James, and John his brother, and bringeth them up into an high mountain apart, And was transfigured before them: and his face did shine as the sun, and his raiment was white as the light.

If you read the whole passage, you can see by the disciple's reaction that this display of his power and glory was not a regular occurrence. This passage proves that he did not operate in his full power, anointing, and glory when he was here.

> John 17:5, KJV
> And now, O Father, glorify thou me with thine own self with the glory which I had with thee before the world was.

Jesus had a glory with the Father that he did not fully or consistently reveal when he was here on earth. So why did he do it this way? Why didn't he come and show us the fullness of all the power and glory that he has? I believe he did it that way to show us how to walk in the power of God. He showed us how we can be highly anointed by God and still live in these fleshly bodies.

Let's look at another passage that always comes up when this topic is discussed.

> John 14:12, KJV
> Verily, verily, I say unto you, He that believeth on me, the works that I do shall he do also; and greater works than these shall he do; because I go unto my Father.

The reason he said in this passage we will do "greater works" is simple. There is no mystery here. He first affirms that the one who believes will do the same works that he has done. This confirms what I have been saying about having faith in God and believing his Word. When we have faith, we will do what Jesus did. Secondly, he is leaving, so his work on earth in that capacity at that time was ending. He is going to the Father, so our works are going to be greater because there are more of us, we are still here, and he is leaving, simple.

I also believe this, the fact that he first came as the Lamb of God, meant that he couldn't display his full power or glory. But when he comes as the Lion, watch out! He's going to come and judge world and destroy the wicked.

> Jeremiah 23:19, KJV
> Behold, a whirlwind of the LORD is gone forth in fury, even a grievous whirlwind: it shall fall grievously upon the head of the wicked.

This passage reminds me of something that the Lord showed me in prayer about the seven Spirits of God. God anoints us with the Holy Spirit just as he anointed Jesus. But we don't have the fullness of the seven Spirits abiding in us the way the Lord does now. When the apostle John saw the Lord he saw him in his glorified state. This does not take away from the power that is available to us through the Holy Ghost. While I was in prayer the Lord showed me a hurricane cloud and a tornado funnel touching down to the earth from that cloud. He showed me the power and force that is demonstrated by that whirlwind or tornado funnel. This is what we have, we don't have the whole cloud, but we have the whirlwind of the Holy Spirit. When the Spirit of Truth touches down, it comes with such power and force that we easily see the works of the devil destroyed. Praise God. Just because we have a desire to have his power does not mean we must demote the Lord so we can get on his level to obtain that power. He has already bought us up to a new level and a new power.

We don't have the fullness individually but we have access to more than enough of the Spirit of God to do the work. We have access to all the power of the seven Spirits of God. I'm going touch on a few points of the access we have and the seven Spirits work in the life of the believer.

- The Spirit of Grace ushers in salvation to us. The five pillars of the Spirit of Grace saves us, helps us pray, enables us in our calling, provides for us, and then when we need it great grace is bestowed upon us. Miracles, power, and deliverance are manifested in the great grace atmosphere.

- The Spirit of Judgment is there when it is necessary to facilitate judgment in our lives. Especially when others cross the line with God's anointed. God will judge the world by the Spirit of Judgment according to his purpose.

- The Spirit of Glory manifests God's glory in our lives. The Spirit of Glory changes us and brings us from glory to glory (2 Cor. 2:18). The Spirit of Glory rests upon us and causes us to shine. The Spirit of Glory is the confirmation of God's presence.

- The Spirit of Life resurrects us spiritually and physically. Without the Spirit of Life we will not be resurrected. The Spirit of Life also resurrects now.

- We know what the Spirit of prophecy does in the life of the believer. Prophecy is supernatural language from heaven. It's also a foretelling of the future. It's also militant; it is one of our spiritual weapons. It's a sword in our mouth to destroy the works of the devil.

- We are filled with the Spirit of Truth. The Spirit of Truth teaches us, comforts and restores us and causes us to walk in God's truth. Of all of the seven Spirits of God, the Spirit of Truth is the one God chose to dwell in the believer and cause us to speak in his heavenly language.

- The Spirit of Wisdom breaks down into six dimensions (Isaiah 11:2). Wisdom, understanding, counsel, might, knowledge and the fear of the Lord. We need the Spirit of Wisdom, revelation, and knowledge. We need the Spirit of Wisdom above all things to access "the exceeding greatness of his power".

Ephesians 1:16-19, KJV
Cease not to give thanks for you, making mention of you in my prayers; That the God of our Lord Jesus Christ, the Father of glory, may give unto you the spirit of wisdom and revelation in the knowledge of him: The eyes of your understanding being enlightened; that ye may know what is the hope of his calling, and what the riches of the glory of his inheritance in the saints, And what [is] the exceeding greatness of his power to us-ward who believe, according to the working of his mighty power,

We must also fast. There are certain types of demonic forces that specifically need prayer and fasting to be conquered in the spirit. Don't just fast, pray and fast so we can have that yoke and bondage breaking faith.

Isaiah 58:6, KJV
[Is] not this the fast that I have chosen? to loose the bands of wickedness, to undo the heavy burdens, and to let the oppressed go free, and that ye break every yoke?

Jesus talked about "great faith" and "little faith". I don't want little faith. I want great faith.

Hebrews 11:6, KJV
But without faith [it is] impossible to please [him]: for he that cometh to God must believe that he is, and [that] he is a rewarder of them that diligently seek him.

As I said earlier, I believe Enoch is a type of the present day believer. Especially, after I read the previous verse. Enoch pleased God by his faith walk. In order for us to please God we must have faith in God. Enoch was raptured and caught up to God. We are waiting for the Lord to rapture us, the overcoming church. I believe this "Enoch" generation is a "strong faith" generation. The Spirit of Truth was given to us so we could walk in the truth. If we walk in the truth, we are walking in Jesus who is the truth. Since Jesus is the truth, when he walked in the power of the Spirit he demonstrated the truth to us. So when we do the truth, we do what Jesus did.

Within the provision of the seven Spirits of God, God our Father has given us everything we need to be victorious. We have no excuse. It's time for us to lay aside our cell phones and stop spending all of our time on them and all the social media outlets and begin to prioritize the things of God in our lives. Then we will begin to see the fruit that God has ordained for us to bear.

God bless you and I pray that this book has inspired you to strive to be the powerful man or woman of God that he has called you to be.

Grace, peace, and blessings,
D. W. Knight

For prayer, speaking engagements, or any other info, please visit www.dwknightministries.com

Printed in the United States
By Bookmasters